SO-BJN-655

What to do
about
performance
appraisal

Marion S. Kellogg

What to do about performance appraisal

Revised Edition

ama
com

A Division of American Management Associations

Library of Congress Cataloging in Publication Data

Kellogg, Marion S
    What to do about performance appraisal.

    Includes bibliographical references.
    1. Employees, Rating of. I. Title.
HF5549.5.R3K42   1975   658.31'25   75-8604
ISBN 0-8144-0538-9

Sixth Printing

preface

ALMOST EVERY COMPANY HAS SOME SORT OF EMPLOYEE AP-
praisal system. For most, managers complete a single form once
or twice yearly. This is supposed to determine pay decisions,
help an employee improve his performance, overcome personality problems, identify his potential for future growth, and
more.

That one piece of paper, no matter how skillfully completed and discussed with the employee, should do all these
things would be nothing short of miraculous. That its patent-
medicine approach seldom does any of these things effectively
is a more realistic statement of fact.

Yet managers do need to make employee appraisals, and
for many purposes. This book is intended as a day-to-day practical guide for the operating manager. It should help him perform his appraisal function with intelligence and common sense
and see it in its proper light—that of serving as a springboard for
dynamic, innovative, well-planned managerial actions.

The admonition of *The Mikado* to "let the punishment fit
the crime" is the theme of these pages. Let the manager look to
the reason for his appraisal and select an instrument designed
for his purpose. Having made his appraisal, let him select and
carry out a course of action that will resolve his problem or
achieve his purpose.

Down with lip service to paperwork systems that lead the
manager to believe he has done his job when he has merely filled
out the form or discussed it with the employee!

Up with managerial responsibility to take action for
needed results—and when this requires appraisal, to make one
on the basis of sound information.

Marion S. Kellogg

introduction to
the revised edition

SINCE 1965, WHEN THE FIRST EDITION OF THIS BOOK WAS WRIT-
ten, many changes have taken place. These changes have occurred not so much in the technology of appraisal, although the
behavioral science information available at that time has been
confirmed and advanced. Rather, the changes have occurred in
our improved understanding of the setting or climate for appraisal and the more nearly equal role of employee and manager
in making and acting upon appraisal judgments.

We are, for example, more aware than ever before of the
importance of the relationship between the appraiser and the
appraised. We have learned quite a bit about the effect of managerial style on growth for both the individual and the organization. We have learned to place new importance on open interaction between employee and manager at the time they reach
agreement on what is to be done, as they proceed to do it, and
finally as they take stock of what has been achieved.

Our perceptions have altered in part because social scientists have contributed new information to the work of managing, in part because of changes in society's workforce itself. But
these changes in no way lessen the need for appraisal judgments. In fact, they reinforce the need for support and imagina-
tion in making sound judgments and decisions and in taking
action.

As new, young employees enter the workforce, they ask
for and deserve more frequent formal feedback from their managers than managers have been accustomed to giving. Minority
and women workers, encouraged to advance as rapidly as possible, also deserve more and better coaching, as do older employees who sometimes feel left out of the mainstream of business and industrial life. In fact, most employees demand greater

voice in defining their jobs, setting their goals, appraising their contribution to organization results, and taking more responsibility for advancing their own careers. Faced with the desire for this high level of employee involvement, managers need to develop skills that both encourage and count on employee initiatives in basic personnel practices.

In the end, however, the manager retains his personal responsibility for achieving organization results. He must decide how to work effectively with each individual in the organization. He must agree on work assignments, rewards, advancement, and similar matters for each employee. He must face the fact that *he* has—or has not—contributed to the growth of the work team. For this reason, employee appraisal remains in large measure an individual managerial concern. True, it is specifically constructed from the information and perceptions of those who know the person's work well, but the decisions upon which the manager acts are uniquely his.

It is to this individual appraisal—and to the determination of appropriate courses of action—that this book continues to address itself.

Two factors are fundamental to all types of appraisal: a description of work commitments agreed to at the beginning of the planning period and the actual accomplishments achieved. Together these provide a significant input for each of the several types of appraisal a manager may be required to make. Suggestions of additional factors to be considered are outlined in the exhibits, which illustrate documentation for each important kind of appraisal.

Finally, lest I be judged as prejudiced against my sisters in the workforce, let me say that solely for ease of reading, the pronoun *he* is generally used for manager and worker. It is meant (as it was meant in 1965) to include both men and women.

M.S.K.

contents

chapter 1

The inevitability
of appraisal

ALL MANAGERS MAKE APPRAISALS OF OTHER PEOPLE—AND
make them frequently.

"As soon as Mr. Walters called me about Jack and
described the job he had in mind for him, I knew I had a
problem. Because this is a job Jack can do easily, and because of
the increase involved, he'll probably jump at the chance to take
it. Where am I going to get a replacement?"

"In the meeting the other day, I found myself comparing
our managers with the other company's representatives. I decided Joan could hold her own very well. But Tom and Frank
didn't really look too good. I ought to do something about it."

"I knew Hal had something on his mind as soon as he

walked in the door wearing that careful, poker-face expression of his. Finally it came out. He isn't satisfied with the progress he's making. The truth is, his sales have been slipping badly and he needs help to turn the situation around.''

Such comments are typical of the almost daily appraisals managers and supervisors make. Since a manager relies on getting work done through other people, his normal day often involves a series of appraisals.

Perhaps he begins by making the rounds of the various activities for which he is responsible, taking a quick check on where major pieces of work stand. He sees employees, gets a story from them on what they are doing, and, on the basis of his knowledge of each of them, decides whether or not a particular work item requires his attention. Back at his own desk, he goes through his mail, making his answers consistent with the kind of individual he is addressing. His assignment of work to employees is based not only on the organization he has established but on the proven ability of individuals as well. The way he gives instructions is consistent with the kind of person he is instructing. The amount of coaching he gives along with the assignment is adapted to the experience and maturity of the employee with whom he is dealing.

If he has visitors during the day, he almost unconsciously sizes them up and adjusts his speech and actions to his estimate of them. In his contacts with his own boss, he organizes his material and presents his information in ways he believes meet with approval. If an employee is up for salary review, he decides whether or not more money is merited. If he has a vacancy in his organization, he weighs the relative qualifications of candidates in order to decide among them.

None of these things is an unusual action. Each is quite standard for a manager. Each involves the deliberate act of appraising another person. An appraisal is not an occasional, chance happening; it is basic to the manager's work and an essential part of his job.

Not all do it equally well, of course. Some managers are

more sensitive to other people, more perceptive in interpreting their responses, gestures, reactions. Some are more deliberate and systematic in making their judgments. But, skillfully or not, consciously or not, the appraisal is made.

THE QUESTION OF MERIT

It has been very popular in the past two decades to argue the merits of appraisal. The noted Douglas McGregor phrased the negative side of the issue well:

> The conventional approach, unless handled with consummate skill and delicacy, constitutes something dangerously close to a violation of the integrity of the personality. Managers are uncomfortable when they are put in the position of "playing God." The respect we hold for the inherent value of the individual leaves us distressed when we must take responsibility for judging the personal worth of a fellow man. Yet the conventional approach to performance appraisal forces us not only to make such judgments and to see them acted upon, but also to communicate them to those we have judged. Small wonder we resist! [1]

Social scientists like Rensis Likert are concerned about its impact on both employees and managers.

> The fundamental flaw in current review procedures is that they compel the superior to behave in a threatening, rejecting, and ego-deflating manner with a sizable proportion of his staff. This pattern of relationship between the superior and the subordinate not only affects the subordinate but also seriously impairs the capacity of the *superior* to function effectively. [2]

[1] Douglas McGregor, "An Uneasy Look at Performance Appraisal," *Harvard Business Review,* May–June 1957, p. 90.
[2] Rensis Likert, "Motivational Approach to Management Development," *Harvard Business Review,* July–August 1959, p. 75.

Some companies like General Electric have found it wanting:

> . . . The results of this original study indicated that a detailed and comprehensive annual appraisal of a subordinate's performance by his manager is decidedly of questionable value. Furthermore, as is certainly the case when the major objective of such a discussion is to motivate the subordinate to improve his performance, the traditional appraisal interview does not do the job.[3]

Harold Mayfield, however, speaking of appraisal and progress review, says: "Now I believe the time has come for a word of reassurance from someone in business who has used these tools over a period of years and found the difficulties largely illusory." [4]

George Rieder sees its limitations but believes "its intent remains valid." He recommends that the practice of appraisal should not be abandoned and asks: "How can we return to successful fundamentals? How can we breathe new life into a misused management tool, using as twin bases our past experience and perceptions of probable futures?" [5]

The question is not whether appraisal is desirable, since it cannot be avoided. Instead the questions are: Appraisal for what purpose? On what basis should the appraisal be made? On whose initiative? What factors should be taken into account? Should it be written down and saved—or not? If saved, forever—or for a year or two? When it involves another person, should it be discussed with that person? Or, perhaps a better question, under what circumstances should it be discussed? How fully and frankly should it be discussed? How can it be discussed so as to strengthen, not impair, working relation-

[3] Herbert H. Meyer, Emanual Kay, and John R. P. French, Jr., "Split Roles in Performance Appraisal," *Harvard Business Review*, January–February 1965, p. 124.

[4] Harold Mayfield, "In Defense of Performance Appraisal," *Harvard Business Review*, March–April 1960, p. 81.

[5] George A. Rieder, "Performance Review—A Mixed Bag," *Harvard Business Review*, July–August 1973, pp. 61–67.

ships? These are the issues to be argued. These are the elements that make appraisal good or bad, effective or ineffective.

The manager who says he doesn't make appraisals any more usually means he doesn't fill out a form labeled "appraisal." He doesn't mean he has stopped appraising his boss, his customers, his associates, his employees, and himself. The manager who says appraisals have been doing more harm than good usually means that his *discussions* with his employees haven't brought about any improvement in their performance or may even have been followed by deterioration of performance. But he probably doesn't mean that from now on he's going to recommend salary increases on the basis of whim or the toss of a coin.

No; fortunately or unfortunately, appraisal is here to stay as an essential part of managerial work. Since this is so, managers should have a good understanding of what appraisal is, how accurate it can be, and what they can realistically expect from the appraisals they make.

TO APPRAISE IS TO EVALUATE

To appraise anything is to set a value on it. In one sense, there is no such thing as a universally accepted value. The value established for a home, for example, will vary depending on whether it is appraised for insurance purposes, for tax purposes, for inheritance purposes, or even for buying as opposed to selling. It will vary considerably if the basis used is cost of design, materials, and labor—or whether surrounding neighborhood, accessibility to transportation, and other environmental factors are taken into account. Even if the purpose and the basic factors are agreed upon, it will still vary with the person who makes the appraisal, because one appraiser will rate certain factors higher than will his associates.

Compared to a person, a home is easy to appraise. What makes a given human being tick and how worthwhile his work is are subjects for much research by social scientists and much controversy among managers. So the manager should discard the notion that his appraisal will be an absolute evaluation with which his associates will all agree. He should recognize instead that his appraisal is a subjective judgment made on the basis of information that is incomplete. He can sharpen his judgment by narrowing down the use he plans to make of his appraisal so the information he needs to obtain is both reduced and focused. He can further sharpen his judgment by making this information as complete and accurate as possible and by excluding irrelevant information from his consideration. He can, in fairness to the person evaluated, share the reason for appraisal, its basis and its use. He can do this well in advance of formal appraisal times.

Even if he does these things, however, the appraisal will remain his subjective interpretation of what the information means. It will reflect his relative rating of various parts of the information, and this will, in turn, reflect and project his own system of values in various ways. For example, a manager who has come up the hard way, without benefit of a college education, may unintentionally overrate the individual who has his Ph.D. Another manager with this background may resent employees who have had educational advantages, may expect more of them than of other employees, and, as a result, be tougher on them in his appraisal.

So subjectivity does limit the validity of a manager's appraisal. On the other hand, the appraisal decision is no different from any other kind of decision he makes. A manager faced with an investment decision looks at information about the market, about his product, about relative costs of different kinds of facilities and tools, and so on, and then makes a subjective interpretation of what all these data mean in terms of the proposed investment. If he distrusts market research data because he is overly conscious of the difficulty of predicting consumer buying, he will read the answer one way. If he is convinced of the soundness of consumer sampling techniques, he may see quite a different picture and make a different decision. Even the engineer faced with a set of product performance data interprets what the data mean on the basis of his own experience. The important thing, of course, is that there is a final objective test of the whole appraisal process: When the manager has acted on the basis of his appraisal, are the actions effective or not? Do they accomplish what he is trying to do?

WHO IS HELPED BY APPRAISAL

Frequently what the manager is trying to do is to influence an employee to make certain decisions, take certain steps, change certain attitudes—at least outwardly. At best, this is a tricky situation. Much management literature implies that the vehicle for doing this is the discussion with the employee about the manager's appraisal. This raises the question: Is the manager's appraisal helpful to the person appraised? Unfortunately there is no certain answer. It may or may not be. The manager who makes an appraisal for himself presumably feels he needs it and so will use it to guide his future actions. If a person asks to have an appraisal made, presumably he also feels a need for it to guide future actions; and if he trusts the appraiser enough to accept his judgment, or if the appraisal contains strong evidence of validity, then presumably he will use it too.

But if an employee is appraised by his manager, there is no general way of knowing whether he feels a need for the appraisal, or whether he trusts the appraiser, or whether he finds the evidence compelling. He will, after all, make his personal decision as to whether to take certain actions or change certain attitudes on his *own* appraisal of the total situation. The information that comes from the manager is only one input; whether it is the overriding one depends on the employee's view of the manager, the relationship between the two, the credibility of the information, and many other situational factors.

John Jones, completely engrossed in product failure problems and with a deadline hanging over him, probably will not welcome the most well-meant discussion of his career development. Mary Smith, on the other hand, faced with an attractive outside offer, may well be extraordinarily receptive. But in both cases the comments of the manager will at best be only one part of the information each will consider in deciding upon future actions.

Joe Scott, new, inexperienced in his job, may want all the help he can get from his boss. Henry Adams, mature, experienced, and with a decidedly unfavorable opinion of what his boss knows about the work he is doing, resents all suggestions and sees them as unwarranted sniping.

So the appraisal a manager makes in the hope of getting the employee to do something can realistically be expected only to provide the *manager* with a guide to his *own* actions. Perhaps the first decision he must make is whether discussion with the employee is the best next action to be taken. If the answer is yes, he is faced with the need for strengthening in himself sound, helpful attitudes, skill in displaying them, sensitivity and respect for the person he is facing, and an awareness of the importance of preserving the self-esteem of the appraised individual.

Every manager faces several situations in which he needs to make an appraisal of an employee, and these will be looked at in some detail. Those most commonly experienced include the *coaching appraisal,* in which the manager appraises the employee's performance in an effort to guide his own actions to help the employee improve his performance; the *career guidance appraisal,* in which the manager appraises the employee's overall abilities in an effort to counsel the employee regarding career plans; the *salary appraisal,* in which the manager appraises the value of the results of the employee's work as a guide to recommending suitable salary action; and the *promotion appraisal,* in which the manager appraises the ability of the employee to do the work of a better, open position.

Appraisal is a necessary part of a manager's work. It is his subjective judgment of the value of an individual's ability to do something. It is most likely to be sound if its purpose is well defined and if it is based on information that is relevant, accurate, and sufficiently complete that no overriding information has been overlooked. It is most likely to be viewed as fair if the employee knows why he is being appraised, what goes into the judgment, and how it will be used. It serves primarily as a guide for the manager's own actions with respect to the individual he appraises. Discussion of his appraisal with an employee serves to provide an input for the employee's own appraisal on which he will, in turn, base his actions.

chapter 2

The ethics of employee appraisal

THERE HAS BEEN A SHIFT IN ATTITUDE CONCERNING THE ETHICS of privacy during the last decade. It leads the sincere, thoughtful manager to ask whether he has a right to make appraisal judgments about his associates. And, more important, has he the right to make use of these judgments in administrative decisions that affect these associates? Invasion of personal privacy is censured today. Does the appraisal situation constitute such an invasion of privacy?

The decision rests on the legitimate role of the manager, known to those who form the working team and accepted by them. A manager has responsibility for achieving results for his firm not at the expense of employees but with their help and through their efforts. To this extent, then, his judgment about performance (although it may at times be imperfect) lies within appropriate ethical boundaries. He does not judge the worth of another human or derogate him for values different from his own. He makes his judgments according to whether the individual is contributing previously agreed-upon results to the total team, that is, whether he is fulfilling his role.

To clarify the appraisal relationship and put it on a sound basis, probably the single most important thing he can do is to communicate at the beginning of a work cycle what judgments he makes about team members and the bases on which he makes his judgments. That way everyone will know in advance the ground rules under which they are working and help formulate them. If a manager conveys his judgments to others, employees have a right to know this, to know for what purpose it is done, and to know precisely what is conveyed on all major points. In any event, discussion of appraisal information with a third party should occur only if that party has a verifiable right to the data. If records are kept of appraisal information, employees should know who keeps them and for how long and who has access to them. They should receive copies of such appraisals if they wish to have them.

A manager frequently operates under great pressure, however. He may mean to keep his appraisal judgments within his rightful purview, but unfortunately the occasions for violation are many. Moreover, the actions he takes based on his judgments may be made under severe time limitations, thus permitting thoughtlessness on his part. For example, he may intend to be clear in his feedback and actually be hurtful. Recognizing, then, the many opportunities to slip inadvertently into unethical practice, let's look at some of the more common ones to suggest an appropriate course of action.

KNOW THE REASON FOR THE APPRAISAL

Manager X is at lunch with his top boss. "What do you think of Joe?" he's asked. Manager X is flattered that his opinion is sought. He launches into a fairly detailed description of Joe's strengths and weaknesses. Regardless of whether the substance of his comments is favorable or not, he is acting unethically since he doesn't know the purpose to which the information is to be put and therefore can judge neither the impact his comments will have nor whether his evaluation is based on sufficient relevant information. The point at issue is why the top boss is considering Joe—for another position, for more money, or merely to decide whether to add him to the guest list for a party. A simple question would permit not only a more ethical response but a sounder, more useful one as well.

APPRAISE ON THE BASIS OF
REPRESENTATIVE INFORMATION

Manager X must choose from among three individuals to fill an opening. Since none of them works for him, he is trying to collect information from current and former managers and from personnel records.

The first person works for a manager who speaks glowingly of him. This is "a great guy, a hard worker, everybody likes him. Just yesterday, he brought in an order no one thought we could get."

The second person has an appraisal in her personnel file. It says, "She is new on her job, needs to learn her way around the organization, needs to improve her knowledge of customers and customer products." This appraisal was written ten years ago.

The third person's manager says that he is "distracted, frequently late in the morning, has so many things on his mind that his work is suffering." Investigation shows that the man's wife is seriously ill and that he has temporary, unusual responsibilities for his children and his home.

Manager X recognizes that to use these ratings alone would be unethical. Information based on incidents either too old or too new does not present a balanced picture of performance on which to base an appraisal. Nor does information based on an atypical work period. Manager X needs to continue his investigations to uncover a more sustained performance picture for each of these persons.

APPRAISE ON THE BASIS OF
SUFFICIENT INFORMATION

The NOP Company has an appraisal system requiring that the manager consolidate information supplied by three raters who are familiar with an employee's performance.

Manager X receives the standard form for a man with whom he has had very little contact. He has heard the employee present a report on solving a troublesome production problem, has received two or three letters or memos from him, and sees him fairly often in the plant cafeteria line. His general impressions are pretty good. When the appraisal form reaches him, he groans. "What a job! Well, I'll just do the best I can." Nowhere does the form ask what opportunity he has had for observing this employee, and it doesn't occur to Manager X to indicate that his information is limited. He feels that all he is required to do is answer the questions as best he can. This earnest desire to do what is asked of him results in unethical conduct. If the man's supervisor gives Manager X's information equal weight with the opinion of others who know this man's work well, then he too is being unethical. A simple refusal to rate the man—or a rating only on what he has observed, with a notation indicating the extent of the observation—would have been not only ethical but also more useful in the circumstances. The fact that the recorded impressions are favorable is not the point at issue.

APPRAISE ON THE BASIS OF
RELEVANT INFORMATION

Joe is being considered for promotion to a job that requires considerable technical knowledge of manufacturing processes and quality control as well as the ability to contact and work with both engineers and the factory superintendent. These represent areas of strength in Joe's past performance. But Joe's boss, Manager X, appraises him as not qualified for the job because he does not have a college degree. Granted that promotion is won on a competitive basis and that others may be better qualified than Joe (with or without degree), nevertheless Manager X's appraisal, if it is truly made on the basis of this one point only, is probably unethical. If the job qualifications are as given, Manager X's basis for appraisal does not appear relevant; at the very least, he should state Joe's qualifications against the job requirements. On the other hand, if Manager X believes that lack of college experience limits Joe's ability to do the job in ways not stated, he should say so. In other words, his appraisal may be sound, but he needs to qualify it so as not to mislead the hiring manager.

MAKE AN HONEST APPRAISAL

Manager X believes that he should speak only favorably of employees. "After all, those who live in glass houses shouldn't throw stones." And so those in his organization invariably have a personnel file full of glowing appraisals. His people can do anything. His people are the best.

It is possible to make only favorable statements about subordinates without being unethical provided the manager is quite exact in what he says. But at least two unfortunate effects are more likely. First, the manager is inclined to overrate employees so that he misleads others who apply his evaluations. Second, as his practice becomes obvious to his associates, his better employees will suffer because those who use his evaluations will be unable to distinguish the better from the poorer performers. The manager who gives an unjustifiably flattering picture of an individual is just as misleading, just as unethical, and just as unfair to an employee as is a manager who gives an unjustifiably unflattering description.

KEEP WRITTEN AND ORAL APPRAISALS CONSISTENT

Manager X is such a kind-hearted gentleman that he cannot bear to hurt an employee. In his discussions of performance he says only complimentary things. When he discusses the employee's future, the picture he paints is rosy indeed. The employee has trouble understanding why his salary does not improve and why he hasn't had a promotion in years. The personnel records, unfortunately, are quite different from the oral evaluations.

It would be hard for Manager X to be more unethical, more misleading, less helpful to employees. If a boss really wants to be kind, what he tells any employee will be consistent with the written record, and both will be as honest and fair as he can make them.

PRESENT APPRAISAL AS OPINION

Joe, who has been with the company for six months, asks his manager to discuss his future with him. He has had another offer, and he would like a better basis for deciding whether to leave or stay.

His manager agrees to the discussion. In the course of it he states that Joe "will never make more than $14,000 or $15,000 in the company" since he is "not an engineer."

Whether Joe stays or goes, the manager's flat statement about Joe's future is unethical as given. The appraisal is short-time. At best, it represents the manager's subjective opinion based on his observation of Joe and of others who have gotten ahead in the company. Speculation about the future is only speculation. The manager is not God; he cannot foresee the events of the next two or three decades. He needs to explain all these things to Joe and give an opinion if he wishes but qualify it so that Joe understands how limited its value may be.

GIVE APPRAISAL INFORMATION ONLY TO THOSE WHO HAVE A RIGHT TO KNOW IT

The response to a strange voice at the other end of the telephone line asking for an appraisal of a present or former employee should be a request for verification of the caller's need to know and the employee's wish to have him know. And even then, it should be limited to fairly simple, factual information.

The casual question, asked at lunch or over cocktails and designed to elicit an appraisal of an employee or associate, should be deferred until a more private moment—and then answered only if the questioner has a legitimate reason for his interest and a right to the information.

DON'T IMPLY THE EXISTENCE OF
AN APPRAISAL THAT HASN'T BEEN MADE

Manager X is about to recommend someone to fill an important job in his organization. He has considered five candidates and believes one is head and shoulders above the others. While he's waiting in his boss's outer office, the secretary tips him off that the boss is thinking of another person whom he has not even considered. Manager X decides to use offensive tactics. When he begins his discussion, he says, "Naturally I had to eliminate a number of individuals for one reason or another, like . . ." and he names several, among them the one he was told about. "I finally narrowed it down to five. . . ." And he goes on with his pitch.

This is unethical. The implication is that the overlooked employee was eliminated for a good reason and does not stack up with the other five. Manager X needs to admit he has not considered the person mentioned and, if his boss insists on adding him or her to the final list, should volunteer to make the required investigation.

In another example of a shabby maneuver, a manager is asked for an appraisal of an individual being considered for a job. He says, in a horrified tone, "You're considering *Helen?* Well, I guess I must disqualify myself from appraising her. I, uh, don't know enough about her." The lasting implication is that what he knows is devastatingly unfavorable, and Helen is probably ruled out of the running not only for this job but for others as well.

Either the manager knows something relevant or not. If

he does, he should say what it is and how he knows it. Implying he has information that he is not stating is just as misleading as stating information that is incorrect.

DON'T ACCEPT ANOTHER'S APPRAISAL
WITHOUT KNOWING THE BASIS FOR IT

Once a year, Manager X reviews the performance and career appraisals of those who report to the managers who report to him. He finds this review an enormous help in considering salary increases or reassignments or shifts in organization. He has a well-thought-through series of questions, and he makes careful notes to remind himself of what has been said.

One manager, he notices, has a tendency to make rather strong general statements about employees. Manager X will be failing his responsibilities if he does not question this manager to determine the information on which he bases his evaluations. By doing this he will be able to estimate when and to what extent the general evaluative statements are likely to be true.

Broad general statements are easy to remember but are subject to ready misinterpretation. To apply them without full appreciation of the incidents or behavior on which they are based is unethical because of the possible impact on the individual himself or on others with whom he is, after all, competing for opportunity, advancement, or favorable notice.

DECIDE ON A RETENTION POLICY
AND ADHERE TO IT

Manager X has just assumed his position. One of his early actions is to review the appraisals of the men and women he has inherited. When he studies the file of one of the employees, he notes only a few appraisals present: one from seven years earlier, one five years old, and one from two years ago. When he investigates the situation, the secretary says no others can be found.

It may be merely faulty administrative procedure, of course, but should those remaining documents prove inconsistent or stress inadequacies that have since been overcome, Manager X may reach conclusions that would adversely affect that employee's work future.

Consistency in document retention is important. To be fair, keep all appraisals or destroy all those over a certain age or keep the last one for each job held.

CONVEY APPRAISAL DATA TO A THIRD PARTY ONLY IF YOU'VE TOLD IT TO THE PERSON

A foreman learned through the grapevine that he had been rejected for a promotion because his manager had stated that he lacked certain qualifications. He was justifiably upset. When he protested, his manager said that he had not wanted to discourage him.

This is a delicate situation, since the manager may not have wished to play God in previous appraisal sessions by making general statements to the effect that the man was not promotable. Ethical principles suggest, however, at least two suitable courses of action. At the regular performance discussion he might have said: "If someone were to ask me *today* if you were qualified for promotion to superintendent, I would say that in my opinion you are not. This is because . . ." and he supplies his reasons. If he has not done this and is approached about an opening, he can delay his answer until he has had time to reach a conclusion and can tactfully tell the foreman about it.

MAKE WRITTEN APPRAISALS AVAILABLE TO EMPLOYEES

Manager X holds an "asking" kind of appraisal discussion; that is, he typically asks the employee to make a self-evaluation. It has many merits. He learns how the employee feels, and when they are in agreement, time can be devoted to building sound action plans. Employees, however, do not see or see only casually what *he* has written. Such written material may be used for administrative purposes in later years. It sometimes comes as a shock to read what has been said.

Especially in these days of high mobility among managers, we can help ourselves to greater openness and understanding by allowing the employee to have a copy of his written appraisal.

PROVIDE RIGHT OF APPEAL

Manager X as the immediate manager believes it is his responsibility to rate the salesmen who report to him. One of the salesmen feels that his performance is being judged too harshly, that his manager does not understand the problems of the territory he covers. He asks to discuss the matter with his manager's boss. If Manager X refuses, he is failing to recognize the limitations of the appraisal tool. He will probably strengthen relationships as well as show himself as desiring to be honest and helpful if he allows this appeal. He should make the arrangements in such a way that he is not shifting his responsibilities to his boss but rather is allowing for an impartial re-examination of the evidence on both sides.

OPEN THE APPRAISAL DOCUMENT
TO EMPLOYEE INPUT

Manager X encounters a serious disagreement with one employee, who feels the judgments made about his contribution and the reasons for deficiencies in performance are overstated and unfair. Manager X takes refuge in the old saw, ''Well, it's my opinion and I have a right to it.'' Since appraisal judgments *are* subjective opinions, often measuring more about the rater than the ratee, good moral and ethical principles suggest that the employee should document his view of the situation and that it should be retained in file along with that of the manager.

All the situations just described are typical, familiar instances in which managers make, discuss, request, or in other ways deal with employee appraisals. They represent, as well, occasions for managers to keep ethical principles in mind and demonstrate their application. The essentials are that the manager set a high value on each person with whom he works;

Manager's Checklist on Employee Appraisal Ethics

1. Know the reason for appraisal.
2. Appraise on the basis of *representative* information.
3. Appraise on the basis of *sufficient* information.
4. Appraise on the basis of *relevant* information.
5. Make an honest appraisal.
6. Keep written and oral appraisals consistent.
7. Present appraisal as opinion.
8. Give appraisal information only to those who have a good reason to know it.
9. Don't imply the existence of an appraisal that hasn't been made.
10. Don't accept another's appraisal without knowing the basis for it.
11. Decide on a retention policy for appraisals and adhere to it.
12. Convey appraisal data to a third party only if you've given it to the person.
13. Make written appraisals available to employees.
14. Provide a right of appeal to employees.
15. Open appraisals to employee input.

recognize his own inadequacy to appraise any aspect of another human being perfectly; understand the possible impact, favorable and unfavorable, of his evaluative judgments; and act accordingly.

chapter 3

Prerequisites to effective appraisal

AN ORGANIZATION MAY INSTALL THE WORLD'S MOST EF-
fective system of appraisals, provide streamlined forms for
documenting judgments, and train managers in the art and the
skill of discussion, but if the man does not show his respect for
the employee, the results will fall short of the mark. And unless
the employee is receptive to feedback, wants to improve, and
feels some sense of dissatisfaction with his work or progress,
efforts to counsel him are unlikely to pay off. These issues are
critical to making appraisal judgments and taking effective action based on them.

SELF-RESPECT, SELF-KNOWLEDGE

In any relationship, one person's lack of respect for the other is usually apparent, although it is not always identified as such. Respect is so important that its presence will surmount many problems and permit the two to function cooperatively. Its absence for whatever reason almost always prevents the two from successful joint efforts. A manager and those who report to him organizationally must work as a team in order to achieve their mission. Hence the critical nature of mutual respect.[1]

To respect others, however, a manager must respect himself. He must accept what he is, understand his own strengths and deficiencies. This self-knowledge or insight is in no case more important than in making appraisal judgments and deciding on implementation. For our view of others is distorted by what we are like and how we see ourselves. Moreover, the confidence we are able to exhibit in others depends on our own self-confidence. To help someone else grow involves risk, and only when our inner security is strong enough are we able to undertake such risks.

Before making appraisal judgments and implementing them, therefore, managers should make an effort both to know themselves better and to foster a team relationship with employees.

Team effort stems from shared objectives for the organization and clarification and understanding of the roles and responsibilities of each member. Within this framework, performance appraisal judgments have more meaning and higher acceptability.

MANAGERIAL STYLE

Issues of managerial attitude and style cannot be ignored. Some managers display a self-interest and ambition that color their words and actions adversely. Others are more

---

[1] As an aid to understanding, see, for example, John H. Zenger and Dale E. Miller, "Building Effective Teams," *Personnel,* March–April 1974.

clearly interested in employee growth and organization achievement. It is not enough to have this interest. Such managers must let others see it and must demonstrate it in their day-to-day actions. If a manager is encouraging and supportive of others, thus displaying confidence in the ability of employees to progress, if he positively stimulates their willingness to take well-calculated risks, he creates a climate for growth and development. In this climate, his appraisals and subsequent discussions and actions with employees have an enriching, counseling character.

If, however, he surrounds them with a climate of criticism, warns them "not to rock the boat," and focuses his and their attention on the gap between what is desired and what was in fact accomplished, he often suppresses or limits growth. Some employees view appraisals in this climate as threatening, and discussions take on a harsh, punitive character.

In a growth climate, the relationship between the two parties is strengthened; there is more likely to be trust and therefore more openness. Managers are often unaware of the climate they create. A third-party professional can be of help in providing feedback on this important matter.

With respect to style, managers in most instances need to undertake self-awareness programs. They should ask themselves these questions and obtain professional help as needed.

- ☐ Do I have a reasonable understanding of how others see me?
- ☐ Do I have the inner confidence to risk growth and development of others?

   Is the organization I manage working as a team—do we understand our mission, are our roles and responsibilities clear?

- ☐ Do I *show* my interest in others and my expectations for high team accomplishment?

If such questions can be answered positively, the manager is ready to build his share of the relationship.

EMPLOYEE'S VIEW OF THE MANAGER

Only if the employee respects the manager's knowledge or know-how in the performance area in which the manager is trying to encourage change and only if he believes the manager is sincerely interested in helping him do a better job is he likely to respond favorably to direct discussion of appraisal and improvement recommendations.

Unfortunately managers frequently tend to overestimate the soundness of the relationship between employees and themselves. This is true not only because a manager's own evaluation of himself is involved but also because employees often hide inner resentment, dislike, disparagement, and other unfavorable attitudes that might hurt them with the boss.

While the relationship between two individuals is necessarily unique, here are a few illustrative, generalized types of relationships.

Case 1. Good give-and-take working relationship. Joe and his boss have worked together long enough to know each other's ways and pretty well accept each other on an "as is" basis. Joe feels his boss knows his job. Joe's manager feels Joe performs well. From time to time, of course, the manager sees things that he feels could be improved. But he has found that he can usually talk them over with Joe, and Joe will try to make the desired changes. Joe, for his part, feels his manager really wants to help him do a better job.

In this situation, which is almost ideal for working together, the manager has a pretty easy time of it. Provided he really has worthwhile suggestions to make to Joe, the chances are good that Joe will make the effort to change and to improve within the limits of his natural abilities and at a rate determined by them.

Case 2. The feared but respected manager. Pete believes his boss knows his job but is a very hard man to work for. He is extremely demanding and expects such perfection that Pete tends to hide his mistakes, his problems, and any obstacles he encounters. In addition, Pete feels his boss is interested only in getting the work done and has little if any interest in Pete himself.

In this situation, in which an employee often gives the impression of hanging on to the manager's every word, it is relatively easy for the manager to convince himself the situation is better than it really is. The best clues to the existence of this kind of relationship are the infrequency of employee-initiated contacts with the manager, the relatively few problems and obstacles described by the employee as needing attention, the few times the employee disagrees with a manager's decision or argues the merit of another course of action, and the occasional, unexpected discovery that work thought to be on target is considerably off schedule.

The manager who suspects this kind of relationship should realize that implementation of his appraisal decisions will probably have to be within the framework of the already existing relationship. Any sudden about face, any sudden approach to the employee on the basis of *helping him*, will undoubtedly be viewed with suspicion. Since, however, the employee does respect his manager's work competence and is a little afraid of him, he will probably accept suggestions and try to put them into practice, particularly if he feels the manager will check up on him later. The manager's suggestions had better be good, however; otherwise the employee may adopt them only as long as the manager is watching.

Case 3. The "nice guy," the slightly incompetent manager. Bill works for a boss everybody likes—a "nice guy." Bill doesn't think much of his boss's technical or management know-how and feels he got where he is primarily because he's a good politician. Bill and his associates frankly find it easy to snow their boss and view his suggestions for their own improvement with something less than respect, although they feel the suggestions represent a sincere effort to help.

The manager in this situation may not be *able*—and may not *want*—to recognize the nature of his relationship with his employees. If he does, however, he may note possible clues in such things as finding out that employees have said they will do one thing but have actually done another; thinking a work situation is in good shape, but hearing from the top manager or an associate that this is not the case; or having employees introduce irrelevant topics at a meeting that take time and attention away from the purpose of the meeting. The most likely way of recognizing the situation, however, is with the help of an objective third party—perhaps a management development specialist or a management consultant.

The manager who detects this relationship needs to face up to the fact that his suggestions for work improvement will probably not carry much weight. Employees will listen to him good-humoredly, make their own appraisal of the worthwhileness of his ideas, discounting the value of his ideas somewhat because of their lack of respect for his competence (except perhaps in getting along with others), and then accept or reject pretty much on the basis of what they feel like doing.

This manager needs to double-check his coaching appraisal decisions to be sure they are sound. Perhaps his own boss can be of help here, or again, the use of a competent management development specialist or an outside consultant may add a great deal to the quality of both his appraisal decisions and their implementation. In all likelihood, discussion of the performance area in need of improvement and possible ways of improving it will not be fruitful, and another form of implementation should be selected.

Case 4. An over-the-hill manager. Tom works for an older manager who is close to retirement. In his younger days he was very successful, and his total career contribution to the firm has been high. At the moment, however, Tom feels he no longer represents current management thinking—his knowledge, skill, and standards of performance belong to another era. Though he considers the manager well-meaning, Tom feels trapped and in the position of taking direction from someone who is, for the most part, no longer qualified to give it.

Many managers in this position are keenly aware of the

existence of this kind of relationship. They may feel the employee's analysis is *wrong* and go on trying to prove that their management judgment is as good as it ever was. Another reaction is to give up on this generation of workers and "let them sink or swim."

Other managers fight awareness of this relationship in spite of such clues as diffident and respectful agreement on almost all matters instead of the more normal, occasional differences of opinion; lack of shared enthusiasm over successes and disappointment over failures; and infrequent questions regarding evaluation of courses of action except as a matter of form.

The soundest assumption that an older manager, close to retirement, can make is probably that his employees feel he is no longer the best person to give them guidance and direction. Whether this assumption is in fact true or not, he should probably avoid face-to-face discussion of performance improvement needs and deliberately choose other ways of implementing his appraisal decisions.

Case 5. The incompetent, disliked manager. Bob works for a manager who is considered ruthless, interested only in getting work out, and possessed of little, if any, knowledge about the work for which he is responsible. Bob is sure he knows more about his job than his manager does. He feels that because of his manager's lack of knowledge he sometimes makes impossible demands and then is unjust in evaluating performance. Bob feels, moreover, that his manager's suggestions are usually worthless or, if they have merit, are given only to make the manager himself look good in the eyes of his superior.

The manager in this situation probably sees it a little differently. Although he is aware that he lacks the specialized knowledge his employees have, he probably feels that his general knowledge of business, business methods, and ways of getting work done are all he needs to do his job.

If he is aware of how employees feel about him, he may believe it makes no difference to the total productivity of the group. If he is unaware of their reaction, such clues as high turnover among his employees, unwillingness on their part to sacrifice personal time in order to get work done, and covering up of mistakes and failures may help him.

In cases such as these, discussion of appraisal conclusions is not likely to be productive. Either the manager should check out what he is expecting of employees with a specialist in the work he is managing or he should give the employees themselves more say in what they are to do. When he sees the need for performance improvement, some method other than discussion should probably be chosen to bring it about.

Note that in each of these cases the employee's perception of the manager's competence and interest in helping him do a better job is the critical factor. Since the manager is admittedly able to get only an imperfect grasp of this view, it will always be safer, when it comes to implementing appraisal decisions, to assume that a poorer relationship exists than may actually be the case.

EMPLOYEE RECEPTIVITY

Clearly there is a strong connection between employee receptivity and employee-manager relationship. If the relationship between the two is poor, the employee will not be receptive even to the most meaningful and well-meant suggestions for his performance improvement.

However, the employee-manager relationship is not the only factor affecting the employee's receptivity, and the manager who seriously wishes to help the employee do a better job needs to be aware of other common determinants. Some of these also contribute to the kind of relationship existing between the two. None of these factors guarantees employee receptivity. The manager should see them as frequent contributors only.

Factor 1. Differences in age and experience. If the employee is considerably older than his boss or has had considerably more experience in doing the assigned work, his receptivity to his manager's suggestions will probably be low. On the other hand, if the manager is a little older than the employee and has had more directly related experience, the employee's receptivity will probably be high.

Factor 2. Rivalry. If the employee expected or hoped to be promoted to the position held by the current manager, his receptivity to suggestions made by the manager chosen in his stead will almost certainly be low—at least in the beginning. If, on the other hand, he was hired from outside the company by his manager or if his manager selected him for promotion to his present job, his receptivity should be high.

Factor 3. Unusual work pressures. When the employee is faced with unusual work demands requiring considerable attention on his part—for example, peak volume of work, changes in work system or method, complex technical problems needing solution, or staffing problems if he supervises others—his receptivity to suggestions from his manager may be low unless they have immediate application to the problem at hand. But when his work is in good shape and there are no unusual pressures, his receptivity should be high.

Factor 4. Health. An employee who does not feel fit for either physical or emotional reasons, and who is concerned about his condition, is not likely to be receptive to a discussion of his performance.

Factor 5. Off-the-job pressures. Unusual family demands, such as illness at home or problems with children, will interfere with receptivity. So will any personal problem that absorbs an employee's attention or causes him worry and anxiety.

Factor 6. Length of time on job. If the employee is relatively new in his position or has just been given a new responsibility, his receptivity is ordinarily high.

Factor 7. Desire for advancement. The employee who is interested in promotion in the near future is more likely to be receptive than the one who has no such ambition.

Factor 8. Recency of salary increase or other recognition. Following a merit increase he views as substantial or some honor that indicates the high regard his manager has for his work, the employee will doubtless accept performance improvement suggestions in good spirit.

Factor 9. Change in managerial attitude. The manager's way of making suggestions may represent a marked change in his attitude toward the employee. Where this is so, the

---

Some Common Factors Affecting Receptivity to Performance Improvement Suggestions

The employee is *more* likely to be receptive to his manager's performance improvement suggestions if:

He feels his manager is competent in these performance areas and wants to help him do a better job.

He is younger than his boss and has had less directly applicable experience.

He was hired or promoted to his present position by his boss.

His work is in good shape and there are no unusual work pressures.

He is new in his position or has just been given a new responsibility.

He is eager for promotion soon.

He has just been rewarded with a merit increase or other honor.

Past experience shows the manager will recognize and reward efforts to follow suggestions.

The employee is *less* likely to be receptive to his manager's performance improvement suggestions if:

He feels his manager is incompetent in these performance areas.

He is older than his boss and has had more directly applicable experience.

He competed for his boss's position and lost.

He is under unusual pressure at work.

His physical or emotional health is not good.

He is faced with unusual off-the-job pressures.

The manager displays a marked change in attitude toward the employee.

Past experience shows the manager has little interest in the employee's response to suggestions.

employee can hardly be blamed if he is not as receptive as he otherwise might be.

Factor 10. Historical managerial actions. If, in the past, the manager has suggested that improvement or change is desirable or has pointed out the need for added knowledge and skill and then has shown little follow-up interest in the employee's efforts to measure up, the employee probably will not welcome further discussion of his shortcomings. But if the manager has recognized and rewarded past efforts, the employee can be expected to cooperate once more to the best of his ability.

If, after considering these ten factors, the manager is still unsure of the employee's receptivity, he can:

☐ *Test it out.* Make a small suggestion and observe the employee's reaction.

☐ *Ask the employee how he feels.* Make a few suggestions for performance improvement and ask the employee whether he is willing to act on them.

☐ *Wait for the employee to ask.* If there is no urgency about the matter, ask the employee to say when he is ready to discuss performance improvement.

☐ *Proceed on the basis of past experience.* If, in the past, the employee has responded well, assume he will this time; otherwise, choose an indirect approach.

Before a manager undertakes serious employee appraisal decisions and actions, he should understand and accept himself to the extent possible. He should recognize both his strengths and his limitations. He should make sure he has taken leadership in welding employees and himself into a team. Within the context of his personal style he should display his commitment to team results and the excellence of all team members. He should test the adequacy and nature of the relationship with an employee who is to be appraised and choose implementation methods and timing that will enhance the person's receptivity.

chapter 4

The coaching appraisal

ALMOST ANY EXPERT ON MANAGEMENT DEVELOPMENT WILL state categorically that managers do not teach or coach employees very well. Yet the fact of the matter is that, whether they recognize it or not, managers do have a substantive impact on employee work habits and practices by virtue of their personal example. The employee sees his manager work in a certain way and tends to follow suit. This is especially true early in the employee's career and appears to persist to some extent throughout his working life. Any group of managers questioned about their practices will almost invariably attribute some of them to former employers who used them or insisted that employees should use them. And since they were successful practices, the managers have continued to use them ever since.

The example is not always positive. Occasionally an employee will say that at one time he worked for a poor manager and saw the adverse effect some of his practices had on the output of employees. As a result, he resolved to avoid certain methods—and has done so. But the point is that as long as a manager is visible to his employees, what he says and does with respect to his own work affects the way the employee tackles his job. This personal example is a powerful way of teaching.

A strong case can be made, however, for additional deliberate and systematic approaches to teaching or coaching that the employee may find directly applicable to getting his work done effectively. When Manager X delegates a piece of work, he does not lose his personal responsibility for the results. The nature of his responsibility has changed, to be sure, but his stake in the results is no less substantial. By delegating this work, he has undertaken a risk. How large or small, of course, depends mainly on the employee's competence to do the job. Manager X manages this risk and carries out his part of the responsibility by making sure that he and the employee agree on the assignment and the results the employee is expected to achieve. He does this by sharing whatever knowledge, skill, or experience he has that might contribute to the successful accomplishment of the assignment; by making sure the employee knows whether he has been successful or not; and by rewarding him to the extent that he has been successful. The employee fulfills his responsibility by applying his full competence to the assignment, seeking help when he needs it, and keeping his manager fully informed about progress. When the manager shares useful information with the employee, and when he responds to the employee's request for needed help, he has opportunities for teaching or coaching.

DAY-TO-DAY FEEDBACK [1]

Perhaps the single most important contribution to excellent performance lies in the informal, day-to-day interaction between an employee and his manager. As an employee works and is observed in action or as he reaches major milestones in his work projects, his manager has a unique opportunity to recognize sound methods, favorable relationships, and useful results. His specific compliments in such areas serve to reinforce his expectations for the worker. They encourage him to continue along the same lines, and because they are rewarding and satisfying to the employee they make such efforts more likely in the future.

Similarly if he observes inadequate performance or work methods or habits or personal relationships, a manager can make immediate recommendations for change. He should point out the negative impact of the employee's actions and suggest more effective alternatives. This early feedback helps the employee discard methods or approaches before they become habitual. And as the manager observes his success in making appropriate changes, he is in a position to compliment the person on his quick response to suggestion, thus making the effort to change a rewarding experience.

New workforce, unfamiliar environment

Frequent, immediate, explicit feedback is of special importance to inexperienced young people entering the workforce. Their knowledge of what is or is not appropriate is limited. Similarly, minority workers whose family backgrounds include little contact with the working world require and deserve deliberate efforts on the manager's part to provide early, adequate feedback. Women and men moving from nonprofessional ranks to professional levels often need this kind of help. Delays in providing such information to "give them a break" are misguided. True tough-mindedness, applied helpfully and

---

[1] See Robert F. Mager and Peter Pipe, *Analyzing Performance Problems,* Lear-Siegler, Inc./Fearon Publishers, Belmont, Calif. 1970

constructively, will in the long run contribute more to these persons, provide for an easier, earlier transition, and certainly bring them earlier success.

Make it explicit but don't nag

Feedback calls for managerial alertness as well as employee interest. For best results, it should be focused on a specific incident or incidents. Language used should be explicit so there is no possibility of misunderstanding. But choose subjects for feedback with care. They should be matters of importance; let the small items go until the big ones are mastered. And don't nag. The point is to make the giving and receiving of feedback a useful, interesting experience for all involved rather than a here-we-go-again event.

Arrange for reports directly to the employee

When dealing with work data as opposed to behavior or methods, managers should arrange for the individual to re-receive first-hand information on results achieved, preferably at the same time as the manager. If results fall below standard, then discussion can be structured around the question "What shall we do to improve results?" rather than on negative evaluative judgments.

AN ORGANIZED APPROACH TO COACHING

The importance of feedback should not be underestimated. It is literally invaluable. It mainly involves *reactive* appraisal judgment, however, based on past work and followed by immediate face-to-face discussion.

There is, however, another significant occasion for coaching. This is more planned, more *forward looking,* more geared to major areas of needed performance improvement. For this appraisal, a more systematic approach is warranted, and a manager needs to organize his thinking and his approach carefully. He makes his appraisal in order to guide his own actions to help employees improve output. It has the enormous advantage that it is designed to prevent inadequate performance and to move an employee toward greater excellence.

This coaching appraisal has four distinct parts. There is, first of all, fact finding; that is, information gathering about the employee's ability—not his ability in general but specifically his ability to accomplish the results the manager is counting on during the six-to-twelve-month period ahead. Second, the manager needs to collect and consider information about things that are likely to happen while the employee will be doing the work—things that may affect the employee's ability to get the work done well. Third, the manager needs to make a fairly objective analysis of what he knows and can do well that he might share, thus adding to the employee's ability to do his work better. On the other hand, the manager needs to consider other sources of knowledge and skill or such additional resources as manpower, money, and facilities that he might recommend or make available to the employee. Fourth, there is decision making or action planning as to *how* the manager can best transmit his personal knowledge or skill or make available other help to the employee. The goals here are to increase the employee's receptivity, discourage his dependency on the manager, and at the same time get better results.

This is not meant to exclude joint problem solving with the employee. Presented here are managerial considerations and actions to help arrive at a decison that coaching is or is not needed. One outcome *may* be a problem-solving session with the employee. But after studying the total situation, the manager may decide that the best help he can supply is, for example, more sophisticated equipment for employee use. A manager, to be an effective coach, must do his homework. What follows describes one way of doing this homework systematically.

THE FOUR STEPS IN THE COACHING APPRAISAL

Each of the four parts of the coaching appraisal is worth further examination. The first part requires the manager to appraise the employee's ability to do future assigned work. The systematic manager therefore begins by listing the major work expected of the employee for an appropriate period of time ahead, usually six to twelve months. To do this he may simply ask himself what he will assign the employee. Or if he has a position description, he may take from it the major responsibilities for which he is holding the employee accountable for the next few months. Or if the work of the department is planned or scheduled, he may take from the department plan the major items the employee will tackle in the next few months. He may make this work list by himself or jointly with the employee, or he may ask the employee to submit his own list, subject to managerial review and approval.

It is important not to list all the work the employee may be doing. The wise manager limits his analysis to a few critical work areas—high leverage points or work where risk is unusually high or items that will lead to major progress.

Since the work list is to be the basis for anticipating how the manager can help the employee do a better job, it should be quite specific. For example, an item such as "Improve customer relationships" for a salesman is less likely to spark constructive suggestions than is "Improve relationships with the

---

Steps in Making a Coaching Appraisal

1. Collect information about the employee's demonstrated ability to perform the work to be assigned in the period ahead.

2. Collect information about anticipated events and other business factors that may affect the employee's ability to do the assigned work.

3. List personal experience applicable to the employee's work, other sources of know-how, possible resources to be made available, and other actions the manager might take to facilitate accomplishment of the employee's work.

4. Choose the performance areas to be improved and select the managerial actions most likely to pay off in improved employee performance.

XYZ Company as a foundation for selling it Product A in the next quarter.'' The first wording conjures up pictures of glad-handing and genial luncheons. Because the second focuses on a particular company and a particular product, it may serve to remind the manager that he knows people in that company, that he knows something of their problems, or that he has access to other people who do. Mention of the specific product opens the door to increasing the employee's store of information about the product and its possible applications to the customer's problems. Use of specific wording also, of course, opens the door to more accurate measurement of performance, thus giving both the employee and the manager a way of knowing how successfully work has been accomplished.

When the work list has been compiled, the manager next reviews the employee's performance with respect to the same or similar items in the past. If the employee has worked for him for some time, the manager may search his memory for past strengths and weaknesses relevant to *the work ahead*. This method is not totally satisfactory since there is a tendency to remember recent events far more clearly than earlier ones, and these may unduly influence his conclusions. There is also a tendency to overgeneralize when one is depending on memory for evaluation material. Ideally a systematic manager, recognizing its importance to the effectiveness of his coaching, antici-

---

Sources of Information About Employee's Work For the Next Three to Six Months

1. Job description or position guide.
2. Work now in progress.
3. Work already committed but not under way.
4. Business, project, or department plans.
5. List of assignments based on manager's best estimate.

**Sources of Information
About Employee's Relevant Past Performance**

1. Manager's memory.
2. Manager's notes on critical performance incidents, favorable and unfavorable.
3. Past performance evaluation forms.
4. Past annotated accomplishment reports.
5. Employee self-appraisal.
6. Evaluations of former managers.
7. Personnel records.
8. Pre-employment checks.

---

pates the need for employee performance evaluation and makes notes of major successes and failures as he observes them.

Many companies have performance appraisal forms that provide for a listing of the employee's responsibilities or work assignments and allow space for notes on how well the employee carried out his responsibilities. If the notes are sufficiently specific, they will provide data for the coaching appraisal. Exhibit 1 * is an example of a good format for recording performance data on a continuing basis.

Another method in use is the employee self-appraisal. Either orally or in writing the employee analyzes what he has done well and not so well on past assignments. The same form (Exhibit 1) may be used for this purpose, supplemented by an accomplishment summary (Exhibit 2). The manager needs to add his own judgments, of course, but if he keeps a record of what the employee gives or tells him, this technique may supply much useful performance evaluation information.

If the employee has not worked for the department long, the manager needs to consult former supervisors for their evaluations and to search personnel records for relevant information. For new employees, pre-employment information may

* All exhibits will be found in a special section at the end of the book.

be useful, and a self-appraisal by the man himself may provide good insights.

From any or all of these sources the manager gathers information and makes notes as they apply against each of the major anticipated *future* work assignments.

Next the manager needs to turn his attention away from the employee and think through events which are scheduled or likely to occur while the employee will be doing the work in question and which may affect his ability to get needed results. Inside the company, for example, are there likely to be changes in organization or people that would have a positive or negative effect? Are there likely to be shifts in business priorities that would influence results? Changes in production schedules? Changes in product design? Outside the company, are market changes expected? Are customer organizations changing? May competitors make certain moves? What sorts of political, governmental, or economic events are anticipated? Again, these thoughts may be the manager's educated guesses, or they may

---

Typical Situational Factors That May Affect Employee's Ability to Do His Work

1. Organization changes.
2. Staffing changes.
3. Employee salary review.
4. Budget changes.
5. Facility bottlenecks.
6. New programs installed.
7. Methods or systems changes.
8. Schedule changes.
9. Design changes.
10. Market changes.
11. Customer changes.
12. Competitive moves.
13. Economic shifts.
14. Changes in laws.
15. Tax structure changes.

result from discussions with his own manager, with his associates, with key marketing people, or with consultants. The manager makes notes of those most likely to affect the employee's ability to get desired results.

Next the manager turns his attention to himself. He looks at each major work item and considers what he knows of the employee's past performance in this or a similar task and the anticipated events outside the employee's control that may make it easier or harder for him to achieve results. Then the manager needs to appraise what he can contribute toward the employee's improved performance: What can he do to clarify the work assignment so that the employee fully understands what is expected of him? Does he possess knowledge or skill that he could pass along to the employee? Is he able to foresee roadblocks or obstacles he can warn the employee about? Can he help devise ways around them? Is there some quiet advance road paving he can do, with or without the employee's knowledge, that may smooth the way and add to the likelihood of getting results? Would an examination with the employee of several different ways of going about a particular task broaden the employee's approach and make him more flexible in overcoming obstacles? Are there manpower, money, or facilities (space, equipment, tools, and so on) resources that it might be wise to contribute at certain points in time and under certain conditions? Can these be anticipated? Can the groundwork be laid for obtaining them? Are there incentives that might be offered the employee if he performs the work well?

Some of this analysis the manager must do for himself, but depending on the relationship between the two, the employee may be able to suggest ways in which the manager can be of help. Industrial relations specialists may be able to make additional suggestions as well as contribute know-how in such matters as devising incentives and preparing for organization changes. Again, next to the important future work items the manager makes notes of ways in which he could contribute directly or indirectly to the employee's improved performance.

Finally the manager (1) reviews the information he has

collected; (2) weighs it as a whole and in the light of his total commitments to his own manager and to other employees; (3) reaches some conclusions regarding the work that is most critical for the employee to accomplish; (4) decides ways in which it is most likely that the employee can upgrade his performance either by himself or with the help of others; and (5) itemizes the specific actions he can take as manager, with or without the knowledge of the employee, to improve the employee's performance.

The way in which these data and conclusions are recorded is of little importance, but sometimes a format is useful to help managers see the full picture. A good summary sheet is shown in Exhibit 3.

Typical Managerial Actions
to Help Employee Improve Performance

With Employee:
1. Clarify work assignment.
2. Clarify results expected.
3. Clarify work standards, measurements.
4. Review likely obstacles and roadblocks and ways around them.
5. Clarify role in and contribution to employee's work.
6. Review alternate ways of getting results.
7. Review progress at suitable milestone points.
8. Contribute relevant personal knowledge.
9. Coach employee to develop needed skills.
10. Share relevant personal experience.

Independently:
1. Provide additional manpower, money, facility and equipment resources.
2. Pave the way through personal contacts.
3. Provide added monetary and other incentives for successful performance.
4. Identify sources of help; provide, as appropriate.
5. Make desirable organization changes.
6. Make methods or systems changes.

Suppose the manager has now completed his coaching appraisal more or less along the lines suggested. Should this be written down and saved? To whom should it be shown? Should it become a part of an employee's record? Should it be discussed with the employee?

For a thorough, systematic effort leading to sound, thoughtful decisions, the appraisal material and conclusions should be in writing. They do not need to be typed in triplicate, but the manager must be able to go back to his notes and refresh his memory. This implies at least a handwritten appraisal.

The appraisal is made, however, to help the manager devise the actions *he* should take to help the employee improve his performance. So it is the manager's document. If the employee contributed to it, it is their joint concern, but it is seldom a matter for record.

The question whether the coaching appraisal should be discussed with the employee is considered in Chapter 5.

Managers make two kinds of coaching appraisals. The first is reactive. The employee performs well and he is praised or recognized; he fails to do something or needs to change how he does it and this is seen and discussed constructively. This immediate, after-the-fact action is called feedback.

The second form is made to help an employee improve his performance on *future* assigned work. It thus helps prevent failure and influences favorable performance. It is based on an analysis of past efforts; anticipated business events outside the employee's control; the manager's own relevant experience; and appropriate actions he might take to facilitate work accomplishment against the actual work the employee will be asked to do during the approximate six-to-twelve-month period ahead. As a result of his analysis he chooses a few critical projects or important responsibilities deserving his attention as well as the performance areas most likely and most profitably to be improved, and he identifies his personal contribution to the accomplishment of the employee's work assignments.

chapter 5

Applying the coaching appraisal

AS A RESULT OF HIS COACHING APPRAISAL, THE MAN-
ager undoubtedly has reached two kinds of basic decisions.
First there are decisions with respect to his personal attention to
specific aspects of the employee's future work: actions the
manager might take to add to the resources available for getting
important tasks done; possible changes in organization, system,
or work process he might institute; and other actions that involve primarily his own thought, planning, and implementation.
Presumably the manager requires little if any help in carrying
out this part of his action plan. Frequently these decisions in
themselves bring about striking increases in the employee's
ability to do his job better.

Then there are decisions about changes and improvements in the *employee's* knowledge, skill, working methods, and so on. It is with respect to these that the manager has to select the best possible vehicle for approaching and involving the employee.[1] He wants to avoid antagonism, resentment, and defensiveness. He wants to encourage constructive thinking, commitment toward improvement, and efficient effort. Essentially he is asking the employee to learn something or to learn how to do something or to learn how to do something better.

How does an adult learn? First he sets a learning goal for himself—what he is to learn. Then he obtains information about the subject. Next he applies the information. Finally he needs to know how successfully he has applied the information (feedback), and if he has not been wholly successful, he needs the opportunity to try again and to find out how successful he will be on the next try. These steps are repeated until he has mastered the subject and has had the satisfaction of meeting his learning goal.

Translating these steps into job terms, the manager's decisions about improvements the employee can make represent learning goals. The task the manager faces, then, is to find a way to (1) move the employee to commit himself to meet these goals, (2) give the employee (or enable him to find for himself) the information he needs in order to make the change or improvement, (3) provide him with opportunities to apply the information, and (4) give him timely and useful feedback on how well he is applying it during each successive try.

For example, suppose the manager feels that John Smith needs to improve customer acceptance of the installation manuals he prepares for new products. The manager must find a vehicle or device or method that will (1) move John to agree that the manuals need improvement and that he will improve them;[2]

[1] See Robert F. Mager and Peter Pipe, *Analyzing Performance Problems,* Lear-Siegler, Inc./Fearon Publishers, Belmont, Calif. 1970.

[2] If the manager is highly critical of John's manual, there is little assurance that his criticism will contribute to John's motivation to improve. See Herbert H. Meyer, Emanuel Kay, and John R. P. French, Jr., "Split Roles in Performance Appraisal," *Harvard Business Review,* January–February 1965. This study suggests that criticism is usually not a motivator for performance improvement.

(2) provide John with information or help him to search out the information that will enable him to make the improvements; (3) give him the chance to write another manual incorporating the improvements; (4) give him feedback on the extent to which he is succeeding—for example, the customer's opinion of the improved manual; (5) let him try again, if necessary and possible.

Here are descriptions of some of the methods the manager may select, together with their advantages and disadvantages.

DISCUSS APPRAISAL WITH EMPLOYEE

If the manager selects this vehicle, he will probably begin by asking John how he feels about his ability to provide adequate customer manuals. He will reinforce John's insight if John recognizes past poor performance in this area. He will add his own judgments if he and John are in disagreement. He will work in a problem-solving fashion with John to develop an action plan for improvement of his manuals so that they receive greater customer acceptance.

This method has certain advantages. It gets the issue out in the open quickly. It lets the employee know where he stands with respect to the performance items discussed and where the manager thinks improvement can profitably be made. In this respect, it fulfills Step 1 in the learning process—suggests learning goals to the employee.

This method has certain disadvantages. It does not insure employee acceptance of the goals. If the relationship between the employee and the manager is poor, if the employee is not in agreement with the manager's judgment and receptive to it, the learning process is never really begun and Steps 2 to 5 are not taken.

The manager needs to do certain follow-up things to make this method work. Either at the time of the discussion or shortly thereafter, the manager must obtain the employee's commitment to the goal, probably by putting it in writing and getting from the employee a plan for working toward it. Next, in order to fulfill Step 2, he has to be sure that the employee's plan includes obtaining information that will help him make the improvement. For example, John might take a college or company course in technical business writing, consult customers, and look at other manuals considered successful. To fulfill Step 3, the timing of the discussion must be such that John will write a manual within a short time and so apply his information quickly. In Step 4, the manager should himself review John's next manual or have some other qualified person review it; or he should be sure that the customer's comments are available so that John has feedback—that is, so that he learns the extent of his success in meeting his goal. And finally, as John continues to apply his new information, it will be helpful if the manager will let John know that his efforts to improve are recognized and appreciated.

It is important to note that even with all these follow-through steps the change in performance will probably be completely successful only if the relationship between the employee and manager is good and if the employee is reasonably receptive to the manager's suggestions.

In summary, the direct appraisal discussion by itself is generally not enough to stimulate change in the employee's performance. The manager must be sure their relationship is such that the employee will be receptive and then must be willing to follow through to encourage the employee's learning.

USE PERSONAL EXAMPLE

If the manager decides to try this method, he will, in this case, prepare an installation manual that he feels meets the customer's standards. He will make sure that what he is doing and thinking is known to John during the work of preparation. He may talk over some of his decisions with John so that John knows not only what he decides but why. He will make sure that John reads and perhaps has a copy of the finished manual and hears customer comment, preferably at first hand.

This method has certain advantages. It provides John

with quite a lot of information about manual writing and good data about the manager's and the customers' standards for it.

This method has certain disadvantages. The manager may not have time enough to prepare a manual or it may not be wise for him to do the specific work he wants the employee to learn more about. Personal example assumes that the manager is able to do the work well and that the employee respects his competence to do so, and neither of these assumptions is always true. In addition, this method does not insure the employee's acceptançe, as *his* learning goal, of what the manager is exemplifying. So again, the learning process may never really begin for the employee. And of course, observing someone else is no substitute for trying something oneself.

The manager needs to do certain additional things to make this method work. He must get the employee to agree to work toward the desired goal. The manager's example, assuming he has the necessary time and competence, becomes the informational input to the employee, who must then have an opportunity within a very short time to try the job for himself. The manager's work, as the model for comparative purposes, provides the employee with feedback on how well he is doing.

In summary, personal example is a powerful tool for teaching if the manager who provides the example is viewed as competent, if he has the time to do the work, and if the employee accepts as his goal the improvement of his work and has the opportunity to try it for himself.

PROVIDE A MODEL

Using this method, the manager draws from his files a previously prepared manual that in his opinion meets requirements and was highly praised by customers. He will review with John the things that make it particularly helpful and will supply John with the customers' notes or remarks if they are available so that he has first-hand contact with their reactions.

This method has certain advantages. John sees what a

good manual looks like and learns his manager's and customers' values. It requires minimum managerial time.

This method has certain disadvantages. It assumes a "good" manual is available, which unfortunately is not always the case. It may not cause John to drawn on his ingenuity to improve; instead he may merely copy the basic features.

The manager needs to do certain additional things to make this method work. He must indicate that the supplied manual is intended only as a starting guide. He needs to point out specific areas where in this instance differences should exist and changes must be made. When John has completed segments, it will also help if the manager reinforces with compliments on good work done and points out any work that still needs upgrading.

In summary, a model is a most useful way of showing an employee what is needed. For work where precedent exists, it is most desirable. For new work, however, there is no model, and the employee and manager are, for all practical purposes, creating a model for others to follow.

DO IT TOGETHER

If John's manager chooses this method, he will probably tell John he is most anxious that the installation manual for such and such a customer be particularly good and will ask John to help him with it. They will have a planning meeting to decide who will do what and when. They will agree to meet at fairly frequent intervals. During these meetings they will look at each other's work, decide on needed revisions, then discuss the next steps to be taken and fix a time for follow-up.

This method has certain advantages. It provides the employee with a learning goal, arranges for informational inputs from the manager, gives the employee the opportunity to try for himself, and provides him with rapid feedback.

This method has certain disadvantages. It assumes that the manager has both time and competence to do the work and that the employee considers the manager competent to do it. These assumptions may not always be true. What is more, such a method may make the employee overly dependent on his manager.

The manager needs to do certain additional things to make this method work. He must make sure that the employee has an early opportunity to do the work by himself with the goal of continuing to improve. Additional feedback from either the manager or the customer will add to the probability of continued success.

In summary, doing the job together is a powerful teaching device, provided the manager has the time and competence to do the work and the employee believes he is competent, and provided also the manager foresees an early opportunity for the employee to do the work himself. This method is particularly appropriate when the performance improvement the manager desires represents new knowledge or skill or a new piece of work. In this event it may be used in connection with a normal part of the employee's job or a special assignment.

HAVE THE EMPLOYEE MAKE A PLAN
AND REVIEW HIS PROGRESS FREQUENTLY

If the manager chooses this method, he will discuss with John the need for an excellent manual and describe what he considers some of its features should be, how it will probably differ from past manuals, and so on. He will then ask John to undertake this job and to prepare a fairly detailed plan for completing it on time. When John has completed his plan, they will go over it carefully, the manager adding his comments and observations. Then, as each major phase of the work is completed, they will review it, the manager making suggestions and indicating his standards.

This method has the same advantages as those listed under "Do It Together."

This method has certain disadvantages. It assumes the

employee views the manager as competent to direct his work. It may also build some dependency in the employee.

The manager needs to do one additional thing to make this method work. He must make sure that the employee has another opportunity to do the work without such close guidance and with the goal of continuing improvement. Feedback, preferably from the customer, will add to the probability of success.

In summary, planning plus review is a powerful teaching device with many advantages and almost no disadvantages. It is particularly appropriate when the performance improvement the manager seeks represents new knowledge and skill or a new piece of work. It may be applied to a normal part of the employee's job or a special assignment.

TEAM THE EMPLOYEE WITH SOMEONE MORE KNOWLEDGEABLE OR SKILLED

If John's manager chooses this method, he will select an employee whom he considers expert at preparing customer installation manuals. He will then ask this employee and John to work together on a specific manual, making it clear that he would like the one they produce to be a model for future manuals, that the "expert" employee is to take a leading role in insuring this, and that John will be asked to do later manuals by himself.

This method has certain advantages. The employee has a learning goal, a good source of information, opportunity to try for himself, and rapid feedback. It is particularly advantageous when the manager is short of time or does not have the personal knowledge or competence—or the employee feels the manager does not have it—to supply the information and feedback the employee needs in order to learn. It is useful whether the task represents a piece of work in need of improvement or a new piece of work to be added to the employee's responsibilities.

This method has certain disadvantages. It represents added cost, since it involves the time of the expert employee and may, of course, detract from his own work. It assumes reasonable cooperation between the two employees. If the expert will not share his knowledge or will not let the employee do much of the work for himself or if the employee does not think the expert knows any more than he does, the learning transfer may not be as great as the manager would like.

The manager needs to do certain additional things to make this method work. Assuming the cost of the expert's time is not excessive, the manager needs to find out, in advance of the assignment, something of the relationship (if any) between the two employees and something of the expert's ability to teach or share information. Also, as the work proceeds the manager needs to (1) review how things are going in an effort to avert problems, (2) make sure each man is doing his share, and (3) see that the work is coming along on schedule and does, indeed, represent the desired improvement.

In summary, teaming is an excellent learning device, especially in a field in which the manager is not himself a specialist. It does assume a reasonable ability on the part of the two employees to work together and therefore requires advance investigation and continuing follow-up. Teaming may, of course, involve more than two individuals, in which case the group is usually known as a task force or study team.

EMPLOY A COMPETENT CONSULTANT TO WORK WITH THE EMPLOYEE

This is a variation of the teaming device just discussed. Instead of teaming John with another employee, a consultant is employed to work along with him.

This method has certain advantages. It gives the employee a learning goal, needed information, opportunity to apply it, and rapid and useful feedback. If the consultant is well known, it gives the employee some prestige to be working with him.

This method has certain disadvantages. Well-known

consultants are likely to be expensive. It is assumed that the manager will select a consultant who is competent not only in his field but also as a teacher and that the employee will see him this way. Yet this is not always the case.

The manager needs to do three additional things to make this method work. He needs to investigate and select a consultant who is competent in the performance area to be improved and is a good teacher. He needs also to lay the groundwork. All the employees involved should understand that the consultant is coming to work on a problem that deserves considerable attention and that the specific employee who will work with him has been chosen so that whatever he has to offer will remain in the firm and will be appropriately adapted and applied later. The assignment should be recognized not as a punishment for poor performance but as an opportunity to learn something of importance. Finally, at intervals the manager needs to review how the work is coming, whether a satisfactory relationship has developed between the consultant and the employee, and whether the desired improvement is indeed being made.

In summary, the use of a consultant can be an excellent learning device, especially in those fields in which the manager is not himself competent. It does require careful selection of the consultant, willingness to accept the expense involved, and some follow-through on the manager's part.

PRESENT PROBLEM TO DIRECTLY REPORTING EMPLOYEES FOR DISCUSSION AND RECOMMENDATIONS

If John's manager chooses this method, either he or John will explain the need for improving customer manuals at a meeting of all the employees who report to him. He will describe the problem as he sees it, outline the customer's reactions, discuss the bad effects a poorly conceived manual has on business, and ask the employees to be prepared with ideas and recommendations the next time they meet. At the next meeting John will make notes of the many discussion points, and afterward he and his manager will review the suggestions and select the ones that appear to have the most merit. John will then be asked to incorporate these in the next manual he prepares.

This method has certain advantages. It provides information from several sources. The group discussion supports the manager's contention that improvement is necessary and possible. The employee's goal is quite specific, and he has a good understanding of its basis. It provides an opportunity for all employees to learn more about one another's work.

This method has certain disadvantages. If this is the only problem presented, it may place John in an unfavorable light. It assumes that the other employees know enough about customer manuals to have good suggestions to offer and that John will accept the best of their suggestions. These assumptions are not always justified.

The manager needs to establish the following conditions in order to make this method work:

☐ The meetings should be accepted routine so that the employees are used to getting together.

☐ The presentation of important problems should also be accepted routine so that no one employee or problem is singled out. Perhaps each employee can, with the help of his manager, select his most serious problem for presentation and discussion.

☐ The employees should have either some background in the problem or some way of gaining knowledge about it so that there is a reasonable chance of getting useful suggestions.

☐ After the meeting the manager should get the employee's agreement to incorporating specific suggestions in the next manual, probably by putting the goal into writing and asking the employee to prepare a plan for reaching the goal.

☐ The manager should be sure that the employee doing the work and those associates who contribute suggestions have an opportunity for feedback, preferably from the customer.

In summary, the use of group discussion to stimulate information is advantageous provided it does not single out one employee as failing in performance and provided the manager follows through after the discussion to be sure that all the learning steps are implemented. It probably operates best if the problem presented is not unique to one employee.

An important variant of this method is to invite a higher-level manager, a manager from another part of the organization, a customer, or some other prestige figure—one who either faces the problem at first hand or has some additional facts about it—to attend the first meeting, describe the problem, and possibly review the suggestions after the discussion. Sometimes this points up the importance of the problem, and the differences in viewpoint and language may have a stimulating effect on employees.

TRY "MUSICAL CHAIRS"

John's manager may choose this method if he feels the reason the manuals are not better is that John doesn't understand the customer's point of view. He may ask John to transfer temporarily to a customer service or customer installation job where he will come into frequent contact with customer personnel and their problems. For true "musical chairs," John will change places with someone in the other organization who will benefit from doing John's job for a time.

This method has one major advantage. It gives John an extraordinarily good exposure to information he needs.

This method has certain disadvantages. The manager loses an employee for at least a short time and has to devote extra attention and time to the employee who takes his place. Further, this method assumes that the information the employee needs is available in the job he takes and that he can learn it and will be able to apply it. This is not always true.

The manager needs to recognize these things. He is making a guess about what the employee needs in order to improve. Since the guess may be wrong, he should view the job change as an investment and should undertake it only if the probable payoff is worth the investment. If the stakes are high, he may want third-party help from his own manager or from a management development specialist or consultant in order to evaluate the total situation and confirm or deny his conclusions. He will increase the chances of the employee's learning the things he wishes him to learn by making sure the employee has accepted them as learning goals, by keeping in touch with the employee to review what he is doing and learning, and, if the employee returns, by providing an early opportunity for him to apply what he has learned.

In summary, "musical chairs," by which we mean the exchange of employees so that they will learn one another's work, is a powerful tool provided the manager is willing to give the needed extra guidance to the new employee, provided the new job really offers something the employee needs to learn and he has the ability to learn it and the opportunity to apply it, and provided the learning payoff is worth the costs of this method.

There are undoubtedly many other devices, as well as variations of those already described, for helping employees make desired improvements in their performance. It is perhaps worthy of note that none except direct discussion of appraisal

---

Steps in the Learning Process
1. Set a specific goal for what is to be learned.
2. Supply information on the subject to be learned.
3. Offer opportunity to apply the information.
4. Provide timely and useful feedback on the success of the application.
5. Repeat the process until the subject is mastered.
6. Reward successful efforts (monetary or nonmonetary).

conclusions requires the manager to say he is dissatisfied with the employee's performance in one way or another. All do, however, involve (1) setting a specific improvement goal that the employee accepts and commits himself to attain, (2) supplying information needed to make the improvement, (3) providing the opportunity for the employee to apply the information, (4) providing a way for the employee to receive timely and useful feedback as to how well he is succeeding, and (5) repeating opportunities to apply and get feedback.

Implicit in the process but worth special attention is the necessity for the employee to feel rewarded for his learning attempts. If he accepts a learning goal and finds himself achieving it, he experiences internal feelings of satisfaction that help spur him on to further attainment. The manager usually increases the desire for improvement by letting the employee know his efforts to improve are recognized and, if he is successful, by giving him additional recognition or reward.

Even the most carefully selected method of encouraging improved performance is not *always* successful. Here are some of the most important conditions under which the manager is likely to bring about improvement:

- ☐ It is within the employee's ability to make the desired improvement.
- ☐ The goal for improvement is specific and measurable.
- ☐ The employee agrees to the goal and commits himself to its achievement.
- ☐ One or two goals for improvement are set rather than a larger number.
- ☐ The goals represent increased knowledge or skill rather than personality changes.
- ☐ The goals represent improvement in something actually required and used in the employee's job.
- ☐ The relationship between the employee and the manager is sound; that is, the employee feels the manager is competent and wishes to help him do his job better.

☐ In the course of trying for the goal, the employee is able to tell how well he is doing, whether or not he is on target.

☐ If the employee has tried before to improve his performance for this manager, he feels his manager was pleased with his efforts to improve—that is, appreciated his trying.

When the manager has selected the method or methods for helping the employee improve his performance and has also identified the steps he can personally take, he may document his coaching action plan in a format something like Exhibit 3 so that he has a way of recording his success or lack of it. There is a wide variety of devices available, but in applying any one of them the manager should be sure that all the steps for encouraging learning are implemented.

chapter 6

Work planning and progress review

TOO MANY MANAGERS CONTENT THEMSELVES WITH AN EM-ployee's performance rather than add to their administrative burden by trying to improve it—unless, of course, it is marginal or failing. But practically all admit there is a mountain of gold to be mined if they can find ways to increase the output of their professional and management employees. Good coaching on their part might just do it. What they need is a way to build coaching into their normal process of working with employees.

Work planning and progress review (described briefly in the preceding chapter) are unusually good ways of doing this. Every competent manager has some plans for the work of the organization he manages. He may not have his plans in writing.

They may not be for a very long period of time ahead. They may not be communicated to anyone. But somehow, this competent manager has in mind what he needs to get done and roughly how he is going to go about it.

Work planning means the process of integrating a manager's plans directly with those of the business or agency he serves. In addition, it means making these plans directly and personally meaningful to employees in his organization. He thus ensures that each sees his role in meeting overall objectives. The first step in this process is putting on paper the results that need to be obtained during a given period of time; identifying major things that need to be done to achieve them; deciding the timing on each; and determining the resources of manpower, money, and equipment needed for their accomplishment. The next step is to obtain commitment for portions of these results from each employee.

The benefits from doing this are obvious. First, the manager can be sure that all the work for which he is accountable is assigned with suitable priorities. Then he can see that the load carried by each employee is consistent with the position he holds, with his talents and abilities, with the amount of time available.

Progress review means the process of taking a look, at suitable points in advance of the final due date, at the desirability of continuing to work toward the agreed-upon results and at what has been accomplished so far. Its benefits, too, are obvious. First of all, it gives the manager some measure of control over the achievement of results. At the time of review he can determine whether they will be early, on time, or late; whether the quality will exceed, equal, or fall short of specifications; and, most important, for what reasons. Armed with this information, he can either change the plans to meet the new conditions or tackle the reasons why work is off schedule, add to available resources, help remove obstacles, or do whatever else is necessary to get back on target.

STEP 1: THE WORK PLAN

Most managers carry through this managing cycle almost intuitively. It is the normal way they work. Since it is basically such a sound process, since managers do use it so frequently, and since it also provides an almost ideal vehicle for making regular coaching appraisals and taking action based on them, it is worth considering both how to do effective work planning and how to use it to help the employee improve his performance.

How does a manager do effective work planning? There are as many variations as there are managers. The description that follows is only one way, and managers need to alter and adapt it to fit their company and their individual styles.

Except in very unusual situations, a manager doesn't plan by himself. Planning requires information, and in most industrial settings the needed information is in the hands of a number of persons—his own boss, his own employees, individuals outside his organization. Wherever it is, he starts by collecting it.

He usually needs information about such current business commitments as orders on the books and status of work in process; additional things his manager expects of him in the foreseeable future; basic responsibilities as outlined in his job description or organization announcement; anticipated market conditions and competitor actions; and foreseeable changes in technology, work processes, organization, or personnel that might affect his organization's work in some way. From all this information, together with whatever signals he can obtain regarding the manpower and money that will most likely be available to him, he decides tentatively on the most important goals for his organization during a specified period. Usually a manager makes this decision with the help of his staff, finding their thinking as well as their early involvement in decision making extraordinarily helpful. The time for which he plans will depend on the kind of business he's in, how complex the technology is, how long the cycle time of his product is, and other pertinent factors. Usually it will be for a one-year period. (The goals are as yet tentative because he needs to verify, through more detailed planning with each reporting employee, that what he plans to do is realistic.)

At this point the manager probably reviews his tentative thinking with his own boss. If the reaction is generally favorable, the manager then begins to individualize the planning in a way designed not only to give him full delegation of work and reasonable control of it but also to provide the opportunity for improving the performance of each professional and management employee.

Individualizing work plans is fundamentally the process of helping each employee repeat the basic activities the manager carried out for himself in setting goals for his total organization. The manager's example is itself a powerful coaching tool. If he has been visible during his own planning, if he has had employees help him collect and analyze information, and if he has shared with them what he is doing and why, as well as the decisions he has reached, he already has a head start.

Setting goals for individual employees may vary all the

Examples of Needed Information for Work Plans

1. Status of current work.
2. Backlog work not yet started.
3. Probable goals of organization and their due dates.
4. Schedules of related work.
5. Manager's expectations.
6. Probable resources available.
7. Anticipated market conditions.
8. Anticipated competitive actions.
9. Foreseeable changes in technology.
10. Foreseeable changes in organization or staffing.
11. Foreseeable changes in work systems or processes.
12. Job description.
13. Organization chart.

way from asking certain of them to recommend, in support of the department goals, what their own goals should be to actually setting the goals for others. Among the factors determining the degree of an employee's contribution are his experience, competence, and maturity; his specialized knowledge; the extent to which he is informed about overall business requirements; and the amount of expected change in his assignment. But in general a manager should (1) be sure the employee has basic information about the business, about the department goals his work will support, about any assignments the manager has already decided he will handle, and about the probable ground rules for manpower and money; (2) discuss the employee's goals, regardless of their origin, to be sure that both manager and employee agree on their meaning, agree that they should be accomplished, and agree on what will constitute successful accomplishment; (3) review together the major steps for accomplishment of the goals so that needed resources are identified and agreed to, the timetable looks reasonable, and the timing will fit the goals of the total organization. This activity, when documented, becomes the broad plan for the employee's work. Exhibit 1 is suitable for use here.

Behavioral issues

Since a plan is only as valuable as the commitment of the employee to achieve it, enlisting positive support and enthusiasm is important. The planning decisions are, one hopes, based on sound, logical thinking. Their ''rightness'' or ''rationality,'' however, does not ensure dedication. A manager increases the chances of dedication if the employee is emotionally as well as logically involved. For this reason, managers should encourage open expression of differing ideas and argument and debate over proper decisions. Ultimately these need, of course, to be resolved, but strong defenses of varying alternatives can be signs of a healthy climate within the department.

If it is possible to allow choice of some sort, either with respect to the goal or the way of achieving it, this is desirable.

Indeed, managers should help employees identify the choices that do exist as well as those closed to them.

Some bargaining or trade-off or concession on both sides will also help stimulate interest and motivation. Goals thus arrived at are frequently said to be "negotiated." [1]

Group planning

It represents in some instances a greater investment of time, but planning in a group setting can also pay off in terms of understanding the problems and viewpoints of others in the organization. It is thus a developmental experience for employees. Their interaction may also be of value in defining individual and group targets and in generating enthusiasm for final decisions.

Psychological contract

Ultimately what an employee and his manager agree to do represents a psychological contract between them. If the work package requires the employee to add to his knowledge, develop his skills, fill an experience gap, or undertake a desired behavior modification, the groundwork for the employee's development is established. And the manager's guidance will contribute not only to organization results but to employee growth as well.

STEP 2: THE PROGRESS REVIEW

When a plan has been made for each employee, the department's goals have been adjusted as necessary, and the work is under way, the next step is to review the progress of the work at various points in time but certainly in advance of critical due dates. Managers usually make such reviews at three-month intervals. Again, there are as many ways of doing this as there are managers. What follows is merely one good way, and mana-

---

[1] For the importance of this skill, see Hugo E. R. Uyterhoeven, "General Managers in the Middle," *Harvard Business Review*, March–April 1972, pp. 75–85.

gers should adapt it to their own company and their own managing style.

The review is set up as an exchange of information between employee and manager leading to decision making with respect to the employee's future work plans and, indirectly, the manager's work plans as well. The manager gathers information about any changes that have occurred in the company's business plans, current commitments, and orders on the books; foreseeable changes in his own responsibilities; changes in the markets, the economy, or budget conditions; and all the other factors that might have an impact on the employee's work. The employee puts together information on the status of the work for which he is responsible; changes in technology, work process, or personnel; probable completion dates compared with schedule; obstacles and problems affecting accomplishments; and similar data that could affect his plan.

The review session consists of a joint appraisal of the total work situation and what to do about it, with emphasis on the latter. Each participant needs to contribute recommendations to the final decision. The employee, for example, may devise a short cut to get work back on schedule; the manager may be able to contribute additional resources to the same end. Essential, however, are three decisions: (1) It is desirable to continue or discontinue to work toward each employee goal, according to all the available evidence; (2) the employee's basic supporting plan will be altered in certain specific ways to carry out this decision; (3) the manager will take certain specific actions in support of the decision and will adjust his department's goals and those of other employees whose work may be affected. This discussion and the decisions reached may be recorded on the original work plan, crossing out and changing dates by hand so that the paper becomes a working document. A copying machine will then ensure that all concerned parties have the same information.

Review sessions are continued throughout the period during which the original plan applies; and when the time comes for new plans, the cycle is repeated. Progress reviews may also be conducted on a group basis. Important but different benefits are obtained, mainly in communication and coordination and in beneficial group interaction.

PLAN SELECTIVELY

A common mistake of managers is to set goals for all the work expected of the employee and ask for written, detailed plans for accomplishing them. This takes a great deal of time and in many instances creates a nonproductive paperwork burden. Normal items of work, routinely performed by employees and for which experience data are available, may be controlled by simply setting standards for them and then ensuring that there is adequate feedback on performance versus standards. Any discussion of deficiencies may then be focused on ways to improve.

Setting goals should be reserved for the few major projects or programs that require considerable innovation or improvement. Detailed planning provides a way of tracking progress, and reviews can be focused on the adjustments needed in future planning phases to assure goal accomplishment.

THE POTENTIAL FOR POSITIVE RESULTS

Granted the effectiveness of this management method, the next question is how the manager gets from the cycle the improvement in performance he seeks from each professional and management employee. Improved work generally stems from one or more of the following:

1. The employee understands better what is expected of him.
2. The employee has better total information relating to his work and is therefore able to make sounder decisions when he is faced with choices.
3. The employee is more committed to certain accomplishments, and so he works harder.
4. The employee has available more suitable

resources—personnel, money, equipment, tools, facilities.

5. Obstacles hampering progress have been removed or reduced.

This is the way the work plan and progress review cycle contributes to each of these results.

The employee understands better what is expected of him. In the exchange of needed information about the business and the anticipated internal and external changes that might affect his ability to perform, the employee's understanding of the importance of his work is enhanced. In reaching agreement with his manager in advance, not only on the goals he is expected to accomplish but also on the ground rules and the major steps to be taken, his understanding of what is expected is considerably improved. He sees not only what he will be doing for some period of time ahead but also what time arrangements he must make and the result his activity is expected to achieve. This, in turn, permits him to make judgments about the adequacy of his work—that is, provides him with continuing feedback as to how he is doing so that he can make necessary adjustments. The progress review sessions further clarify the manager's expectations and afford a natural opportunity for him to provide additional feedback.

The employee has better total information about his work. If, through his work plan, the employee sees how his work supports the department and how it fits with the work of others in the department, his timing, priority, and other work decisions should be sounder, and he is more likely to take the initiative in establishing good working relationships with employees doing related work.

The employee is more involved and committed. The presence of a written personal goal, especially one to which he has contributed, has a motivational effect on an employee. If, in addition, he understands the importance of achieving the goal and recognizes the extent to which his associates depend on its accomplishment, his motivation is heightened. Further, if he publicly agrees to both the goal and its completion date, there is considerable self-generated pressure to do what he has promised.

The employee has more adequate resources. If the employee's plan is overly optimistic or if unexpected factors enter the picture, the manager has a built-in opportunity to learn about this at the progress review session and can make available additional resources—money, manpower, equipment, facilities—if the additional investment appears desirable.

Obstacles hampering progress have been removed or reduced. During the review process the manager has a natural opportunity to acquaint himself with obstacles or problems the employee is experiencing. He therefore has the opportunity to do something about them. He may take certain action himself, or he may be able to point out ways of minimizing or circumventing the obstacles. And, provided the review is held sufficiently in advance of critical due dates, he is able to do this before any damaging effect on the employee's work is irreparable.

The process provides the manager with a chance for making coaching appraisals and putting his appraisals to work. Earlier we said the first step in making such an appraisal is to identify the work the employee would be doing in the months ahead. The work plan gives the manager this information. The second step is to consider trends in the employee's performance so as to select one or more that might be worked on profitably. In the work planning and progress review system, this kind of information usually comes out of the review session in a meaningful way. The third step is to pinpoint situational factors, internal or external, that might affect the employee's work. The manager gets these data in preparing for his total organization planning and from the information he exchanged with the employee to help him make his own plans. As a fourth step, the manager is supposed to identify things he knows or knows how to do that he might pass along to the employee or actions he might himself take to facilitate performance. This is hard to do in the abstract, but when the state of the work is discussed in the review sessions, he is able to contribute from his own knowledge and experience and see ways to be of help.

Moreover, the two-step process of work planning and progress review bridges the gap between appraisal and action. During review sessions, the manager is able to communicate on the spot anything he believes could help the employee. As he recognizes experience or skill deficiencies in the employee's career, he is able to incorporate these into the next set of goals established. Decisions as to administrative action he might himself take (such as changes in organization, in work systems, or in resource allocation), flowing as they do from discussion of work obstacles, can usually be implemented with greater certainty that the employee understands the need for them, will be receptive to them, and will cooperate in making them a success.

EXAMPLE: THE PLANT EMPLOYMENT MANAGER

As an example of the work planning and progress review process, take the case of a plant employment manager who wishes to bring about an improvement in the performance of an engineering recruiter who reports to him.

Information collection and organization goal setting. The employment manager begins by gathering information regarding the number of open positions currently on the books, the expected manpower needs of managers in the plant for the next six months, the broad classification or backgrounds of personnel needed, and the probable timing of manpower needs. He consults with the sales manager and the accounting manager to determine whether the sales forecast and total budget bear out his predictions. Employees reporting to him supply him with data on the difficulty of hiring various types of personnel, the need to go outside the plant community, the probable turnover, and similar problems. On this information he bases the goals for his total organization. One of these goals, which he assigns to the engineering recruiter, is to recruit 20 engineers during the next six months. The manager's boss agrees this number is in the right ball park.

Setting the stage. The employment manager then shares the relevant information with the engineering recruiter, gives him some idea of the money available to do the recruiting, and asks him to recommend goals for his work over the next six months.

The engineering recruiter adds to the information. He consults with his normal sources of supply for engineers, looks at current and projected advertising costs and agency fees, perhaps adds such specifics as backgrounds desired in the new recruits, considers the backlog of open requests and past problems that might recur, and finally prepares a recommendation for the approval of his manager.

Individual goal setting. The employment manager and the engineering recruiter then discuss pertinent considerations—the number of recruits needed, the cost, the reasons for the cost, the time for the recruiting and why, the various ways the recruiting might be done—and finally agree on 20 engineers of specified backgrounds to be obtained at specified times at a specified total cost. The dollars and times may represent some compromises with the original ground rules suggested by the manager.

The engineering recruiter, however, has several additional goals to propose for his own work. One of these is to improve his own interviewing skill and to document in more detail the information learned during interviews with promising candidates. A second goal is to help the managers who will make the hiring decisions to improve their interviewing skills and their documentation of information obtained.

As the manager and the engineering recruiter discuss these additional goals, the manager is reminded of something he feels would improve recruiting performance; that is to say, a better follow-up program six months after hiring to determine the adequacy of each man for the job for which he was hired and the extent to which each is satisfied and challenged by the job now that he is in it. He suggests this to the recruiter, they agree it would be a helpful addition to the total program, and it is added to the list of goals.

When the employment manager has followed this goal-setting process with each person reporting to him, made whatever internal adjustments are necessary for coordination purposes, and reviewed the important goals with his own boss and any others whose work or work results may be affected, the goals, with due dates and necessary resources, are put into writing and considered firm.

Detailed planning. The manager then asks each of his reporting employees to map out the major steps or tasks they will undertake in order to reach their agreed-upon goals. In the case of the engineering recruiter, he may detail these for only one or two months ahead, since considerable adjustment may be necessary if the plan does not bring in enough qualified technical personnel. Basically he decides how much of the budget will be allocated to advertising, how much to agency fees or consulting firm fees, what recruiting trips will be taken to other cities, what technical meetings will be attended, and so on. He predicts the number and kind of professionals who will be recruited as a result of each step.

As for the interview improvement goal, he decides on a course he will take and then, in turn, give to hiring managers, and he schedules the times for these activities. He also allocates time for preparation of an interview documentation form and a communication program for introducing it and selling it to potential users.

Finally, he schedules time for devising his follow-up program, and he decides the date on which he will initiate it.

The engineering recruiter then presents these plans to his manager. As they discuss how the goals will be accomplished, the manager is reminded of a number of points worth discussion. For example, he reviews his feelings about what kind of advertising he thinks enhances the company image and what kind does not. The two also reach agreement on how to handle applications from customers and other community firms. They want to maintain cordial relations with these companies; at the same time they have to protect the right of the individual to seek new employment if he chooses. The manager makes a note to pave the way for the new hires' follow-up program by presenting it to the plant manager and those who report to him and, in addition, to schedule a more detailed presentation by the engineering recruiter a little closer to the time the program will begin.

The manager makes it clear to the recruiter that his performance will be measured primarily by the extent to which he actually recruits qualified engineers on time and within the budget. The improved interviewing and documentation and the follow-up program as well will be judged negatively for the time being—that is, the recruiter's performance will be considered satisfactory insofar as other managers do not object to the added documentation burden or to the follow-up with new hires. Later these "measures" will be refined.

Notes are made of the decisions or conclusions reached during the discussion—a process that is repeated with each of the reporting employees.

Preparation for progress review. After an appropriate time interval, the manager and the recruiter sit down to review progress. This may be done just after completion of a major task or step; or in the case of short-range, continuing work, at the end of a month; or in the case of long-range work, at the end of three months.

The manager prepares for this discussion by rechecking the information originally obtained as a basis for goal setting. If he finds it is no longer accurate, he determines what changes have occurred that may affect the work of his organization. The employee also rechecks his original information and puts together data that indicate whether his work is on schedule and, if not, what might be done about it.

Progress review discussion. The manager schedules his

discussion with the engineering recruiter about six weeks after the start of recruiting. This gives enough time to get the first month's results. In rechecking his information, the manager learns that business is exceeding expectations and that the recruiting schedule will probably need to be stepped up later in the year. He also finds that one manager is disgruntled because he has not hired any new engineers.

At the beginning of the discussion the manager asks the recruiter to brief him on where the work stands. The recruiter reports that he is on schedule so far as numbers are concerned but that recruits have not been obtained according to the priority system for open jobs. He shows the manager a new chart he has developed for depicting graphically which managers are interviewing prospective recruits and for which managers offers are made so that he can control placements better. The manager does not need to bring up the disgruntlement of the one manager since he knows the recruiter is aware of the problem and is satisfied that the steps taken will correct the situation. He does make a note to check this item next month.

The manager learns that money is being spent ahead of schedule, however, and that there is no really adequate plan for reducing expenditures. Together he and the recruiter review all the ways of reducing costs they can think of, and they decide finally on an in-plant employee referral program whereby employees will be asked to suggest prospective candidates for open positions. This has certain administrative problems connected with it but might be a less expensive method of recruiting excellent workers than some now in use. The recruiter's plan is altered to reflect this change, and both people promise themselves to check the money situation carefully next month.

In this fashion, the discussion continues through the most important work scheduled for the elapsed time period, accomplishment is looked at against the final goal, and changes are made to reflect performance to date and also to incorporate expected business changes. Notes are made of conclusions and decisions, and a time is set for the next progress review.

The manager holds a similar discussion with each employee reporting to him. The emphasis is almost entirely on the work—how to make it better and how to deal with business changes that may affect it. If the work of the reporting employees is interrelated, the manager may hold *group* progress review sessions at least some of the time.

The result in most cases is a constructive discussion, mutually helpful, supporting a sound relationship between employee and manager.

The work planning and progress review is a process by which a manager and an employee reach agreement on the goals the employee is to achieve, their importance to the work of the organization, the ground rules to be observed, and the major steps to be taken toward them. Progress against these goals is reviewed at frequent intervals in an effort to keep needed work on target.

Thoughtful use of this cycle, which most managers follow to some extent in any case, provides an excellent vehicle for building in natural opportunities for the manager to make coaching appraisals and put them to work to help employees improve their performance.

chapter 7

What about personality?

MANAGERS WHO FEEL COMPLETELY CONFIDENT ABOUT THEIR ability to coach employees to do almost anything often feel defenseless in the face of personality problems. "What shall I do about the man who steps on everybody's toes?" "What about the tremendously capable engineer who is just too shy to defend his designs against criticism?" It's questions like these that frequently disturb managers and on which they seek help.

While such problems are not insurmountable, the road to improvement is a long, difficult one. The manager who starts down it should know that the chances of success are few and that at best he should expect only modest improvement.

ALTERNATIVE METHODS OF APPROACH

As a starting point, the manager might reflect on the reasons why he has reached the conclusion that an employee's deficiencies stem from a personality problem. If he simply has rated the employee against a set of personality characteristics so that his attention was focused on personality, there is a ray of hope. He may be able to change the basis of his rating and rephrase the problem in job performance terms, subject to standard knowledge and skill coaching techniques. For example, if he rates an employee on ingenuity, analytical ability, dependability, and facility in getting along with others, he is practically certain to rate some items lower than others, and it is quite natural that he will then try to direct his coaching toward improving the less favorably rated points—perhaps the person's ingenuity and ability to get along with others. This presents a very difficult task.

If, on the other hand, he focuses on the employee's work and what parts of it have been done well or poorly, he may be far better equipped to handle the situation. For example, he may find that Helen's ability to do research is excellent and that she has obtained much needed information from her basic experiments; however, her ability to see the application of the information and to get others to see it and use it has not been good. On the basis of this appraisal, the manager can try almost any one of the coaching methods outlined earlier. He can, for instance, try specialized application-type assignments under closer supervision, or he can team Helen with someone else who possesses application ability and see whether close association will improve the situation. The point is that as long as the manager thinks—and appraises—in terms of personality characteristics, he is likely to pinpoint personality problems. But if he can force himself to think in job terms, he may be able to reduce the solutions or attempts at solution to these terms and do his coaching as he would for any needed knowledge or skill improvement.

If, in spite of changing the basis of his appraisal, the manager remains convinced that performance deficiencies are rooted in a personality difficulty, he may, as a next step, try working with the employee to avoid exposing this trait in the course of carrying out his responsibilities. Instead of focusing on the inadequacy, the manager should list the employee's personality assets and focus their joint attention on trying to get the job done—and done effectively—through the areas of strength. Surely there is more than one way to do a job, and it behooves both parties to apply their innovative talents to figuring out how this employee, with this set of assets or strengths, can best get the required results. This in no sense relieves the employee of his responsibilities; it simply means that employee and manager work together to devise different ways of handling responsibilities—ways that do not require the employee to do things he or she is not good at doing. It does imply that the manager is flexible about the *way* in which the work is done and that the employee is sufficiently strong and capable of contributing—and is worth the effort of this approach.

As an example, suppose the employee's problem is that he is just not detail-minded and so, in the job evaluation area, he often makes numerical errors in applying the evaluation grid and comes up with level or grade decisions that are not sound. On the other hand, he is excellent at working with other people and has been a very good salesman for the salary plan installed a few years ago.

There are a number of possible courses of action that might get the job evaluation problem solved. The evaluation grid might be programed on the company's computer so that the machine will take most of the burden for the detail work. Or the decision might be made to permit managers to set their own grades or levels after a training-and-trial period—subject to periodic review and audit—and make the employee responsible for their training and audit. Or the clerk already assigned to the salary and wage department might be trained to take over the numerical work. Or the manager might decide that others in the department ought to be given some broadening experience in salary and wage administration, and he might assign each, in turn, to do some of the work under the guidance of the responsible employee.

True, none of those actions eliminates the employee's lack of detail-mindedness, but the manager's objective is, after all, to get needed results, not to change the employee. He can fulfill his responsibility toward the worker by letting him know that he is considered to be handicapped for certain jobs by his lack of detail-mindedness. The employee can then choose to improve himself in this area if he wishes or select his future positions with this weakness in mind.

Let's take another example. Suppose the employee's problem is that he is blunt and tactless—he lacks sensitivity to other people and seems to offend them in almost everything he does. The manager might have the employee review all the things he normally does that involve personal contact with other people. Perhaps some of these contacts could be eliminated by putting more things in writing; perhaps a clerk or secretary could convey messages to her counterparts in other parts of the organization; and so on.

The point is, does the *job* require the contact or does the *manager* feel the employee should do the job via the personal-contact route? If it's the manager's choice of method, a little flexibility on his part may enable the employee to find other ways that work better for him and allow him to do the job most effectively *his* way. Again, the assumption is that the employee's contribution is worth the effort.

If, after considering both these courses of action, it is the manager's decision that the job *requires* the employee to draw on personality characteristics that are not suitable for the task or to display characteristics that are no asset, the manager is faced with the task of helping him change in certain ways and so enabling him to continue in the position. This must, of course, be the employee's desire as well.

THE STRUCTURE OF PERSONALITY

Let's back up for a moment and take another look at the problem facing the manager.

What is meant by personality, first of all? Personality is the basic set of characteristics that marks off one person from another. It is what one person is like compared with anyone else. Each personality is unique—no one is *exactly* like anyone else. Each personality is dynamic; each is based on certain inherited characteristics that grow, mature, and modify because of the experiences to which the person is subjected throughout his life. Psychologists tell us that, although there is some change in personality characteristics, particularly early in life when experiences make a greater impact, there is seldom a really radical change.

We are talking here about the basic structure of the person, the abiding characteristics that determine his consistent behavior. We are not talking about transient behavior, influenced by a particular short-term situation.

This structure shows itself to others in the way the person typically reacts and behaves in various situations. As most individuals mature they learn to conceal some of their normal reactions and to behave in certain ways because they find these ways are more acceptable than others or permit more adequate coping with life situations.

So, while managers are wise to leave the basic personality structure alone, there is possibility of improvement in behavior, particularly in younger employees; and this is the area that can be tackled with tact and understanding if a manager (1) understands what would be better or more acceptable behavior on the individual's part, (2) develops skill in helping the individual acquire it, and (3) gains the employee's cooperation in making the changes.

TO ACCOMPLISH CHANGE IN BEHAVIOR

It will help here if the manager will once more review the basic steps in the learning process and adapt them to the problem of behavioral change.

Step 1. Set a learning goal. When the goal to be accepted by the employee represents a change in his behavior (even though it is on-the-job behavior) and when the reason for

the behavior change stems from a basic personality charac-
teristic, the manager has a more difficult time than usual in
obtaining employee agreement. First of all, the employee is
much less likely to be receptive since the suggestion of behavior
change may be personally threatening. After all, he behaves as
he does because this is the way he has learned to cope with
certain situations. To ask him to cope differently may be asking
a very difficult thing. Second, in all probability the recurring
behavior is a habit, and for adults a long-standing habit is hard to
break. Third, he may not accept his manager as competent to
judge in this matter—or at any rate competent to help him
change—and if so, the chances of achieving the change are
correspondingly lowered.

Perhaps the most important thing the manager can do is
to be an accurate observer of what situations bring about the
unfavorable or unacceptable behavior and precisely how the
employee responds—what he says, how he looks, what gestures he uses, what actions he takes—so that in discussing the
subject with the employee he can be quite specific. In addition,
he needs to note what undesirable effects the employee's behavior has on other people or on events. Prepared with this
information, he then needs to think through several alternate
ways the employee might have behaved, ways that he feels
would be more successful or would produce a more favorable
response.

Many managers are poorly equipped for this task. Fortunately, in recent years, assessment centers [1] have gained wider
acceptance in business and industry. A manager serving on the
staff of such a center is taught human behavior and its effects on
others and practices observing it. He begins not only to see it
more factually but to describe it in terms that have meaning to
others. This skill is of great importance in working with an
employee.

If, however, a manager feels inadequate to the task,

[1] For a description of this approach, see R. B. Finkle and W. S. Jones,
Assessing Corporate Talent, John Wiley & Sons, Inc., New York, 1970.

fearing he may be tactless or put the employee on the defensive and make him reject the whole idea, it is often wise to call on a third, more objective party. This may be a competent individual from the employee relations staff, an administrative person who is good at working with people, or a consulting psychologist if one is available. As a rule he should not, of course, be a working associate of the employee. In any case, he may be able to help by making suggestions on how to approach the individual, describing behavior in simple terms, and making constructive suggestions for improvement.

Once the manager has prepared himself, with or without the help of another person, he should schedule some quiet time with the employee. Unless there is extreme urgency, it is best to tackle the problem slowly, in several steps and without a time-table in the usual sense.

The first discussion may be only a brief one—20 or 30 minutes—in which the manager says he has noticed one or two things he would like to discuss with the employee so that *he* can start thinking about them, too. He then describes two or three incidents that are representative—what the employee did that could be improved and the effect it had on the other person or on subsequent events. He should especially avoid such generalities and labels as "I feel you didn't show enough initiative," or "You just don't get along with people." Instead he should make such comments as "In the meeting the other day, when I described a problem which was really in your area of responsibility, you said nothing. So Joe picked up the ball and volunteered a number of activities. The result was awkward for all concerned. I was in the position of either taking the matter away from Joe and giving it to you or leaving it with Joe, thus cutting into your territory." Or: "The other day you took some urgently needed drawings to the drafting room, completely bypassed the drafting supervisor, and asked one of the draftsmen to get the drawings revised for you. The draftsman, of course, had other work to do and was mad because he was given more work; the supervisor was mad because you didn't recognize his authority; and the upshot was that the drawings were quite late in getting done.'' A quiet, matter-of-fact tone, coupled with a reasonably direct, factual approach, is probably best. Awkward, embarrassed stumbling around does not help the situation at all.

Then, perhaps having described one or two incidents bearing on the same point, the manager may say something to this effect: ''Now I know you didn't intend that to happen. You were as disappointed as I. So the main thing is for both of us to consider this a little. When you've given it a little thought, let's talk again and see if we can't find out what you could do to help yourself in future situations of this sort.'' Unless the person really seems to be in a constructive frame of mind and *wants to think about how to improve,* the meeting should probably be closed at this point. If the employee appears to want to go back over the incidents and explain why he behaved as he did, the manager may have to be a sympathetic listener for a while just to let him get it all off his chest. But he should avoid the slightest hint of excusing the behavior. In any event, at least the approximate date for the next meeting should be set before the employee leaves.

Step 2. Provide needed information. At the next meeting, the manager might begin by asking the employee if he has thought about the matter and has any suggestions about what he ought to do differently. The manager's tone of voice should assume that the employee *will* have thought things over and will have suggestions. If the employee does, in fact, have an idea, here is an implication that the goal has been accepted. The manager's response should be warm, accepting. ''Good! That might work. . . . Anything else?''

If the employee has no suggestions, the manager may have to offer one as a starter. He will, of course, contribute any he has thought of as the discussion progresses if they are sound or at least sounder than those proffered by the employee. This discussion supplies a great deal of the needed informational input to the employee, although some of the suggestions may involve further reading, study, or consultation with others. In any event, if the employee agrees to try one or two of the suggestions—either his own or his manager's—there is at least surface acceptance of the goal and some knowledge of a way of starting toward it.

Step 3. Provide opportunity for application. Depending on the employee, it may be wise for the manager to anticipate an occasion when the employee will be able to try out the suggestions. It should occur reasonably soon after the discussion so that the employee remembers the specifics of what he is trying to do.

Step 4. Insure useful, timely feedback. As the manager observes the employee's efforts to change his behavior, he should let the employee know his efforts are recognized and appreciated. Whatever represents improvement should be reinforced by telling the employee it is good. Where the manager sees some deficiency, he should tactfully point it out and either reiterate the better way of behavior discussed earlier or suggest a new one. Ideally the goal should be to draw out the employee's own analysis of what he did that was adequate or inadequate and reinforce it if it is accurate, adding an occasional thought where possible.

Step 5. Provide opportunity to repeat application with feedback. Essentially Steps 3 and 4 should be repeated, hopefully with greater success.

THE PROSPECTS FOR SUCCESS

This process will not guarantee success. It merely increases the chances that the employee will be able to change his behavior. If substantial progress is achieved, the manager might then go on to another behavior area where he would like to see improvement. But since the process is difficult and painful for both participants, it is best to take one behavior target at a time.

If no progress is made, the manager and the employee might work out ways of responding or reacting other than the ones originally agreed on in Step 2. But after several tries, if there is not much improvement, the manager should perhaps recognize that the employee cannot or will not change in certain respects and then face the problem realistically—either the employee's total contribution makes living with the deficiency worthwhile or the total contribution does not warrant his continuation in the job.

Often, when managers talk about personality problems they would like to correct, they have in mind very specific disciplinary problems such as frequent tardiness, absenteeism, and excessive personal business on company time. It should be obvious that such shortcomings are considerably easier to deal with than are improvement in analytical ability, development of a "take charge" attitude, and similar more basic traits. Frequently it is enough for the manager to call a problem to the attention of the employee, let him know his current work habits are not acceptable, and request a change. In most cases the manager should inquire into the reason for the lateness or the frequent absences, since a frank discussion may shed considerable light on the employee's feelings about his work, his feeling of importance, and his career goals as well as external situations that may be making it easy or hard for him to do his work well.

In any event, application of the steps in the learning process works as well in handling disciplinary matters as in effecting a more basic behavioral change—if not better.

EMPLOYEE–MANAGER INTERACTION NOT ALWAYS BEST

The burden of changing personal traits or, rather, their expression in on-the-job behavior is not solely that of the manager. He may be the person best equipped to observe and recognize the usefulness of certain changes. But he may not be ideal as the person to trigger the change even if the relationship between the two parties is quite open.

Personal change requires insight and willingness to risk change. The power in the relationship between a person and his boss may inhibit both. Fortunately in recent years great progress has been made in the use of group dynamics to help individuals increase their self-awareness in relation to associates. Sensitivity training,[2] personal style evaluation,[3] encounter groups, team building,[4] and other organization development methods have been brought into more common usage. For complex cases, their potential for helping an employee modify behavior is considerably higher than managerial counseling alone.

No manager can feel he has fully discharged his responsibility until he has employed both the discussion and feedback techniques and referred the employee to some form of group interaction program conducted by a knowledgeable professional.

A manager's ability to help an employee change his on-the-job behavior is quite limited. He should try to express the desired change in work terms so that typical coaching practices may be helpful. Perhaps he can work with the employee to devise ways of getting the work done that do not depend on personality characteristics the employee lacks. If neither of these produces the desired result, the manager should apply the steps in the learning process, being quite specific about the particular behavior he feels is unsuitable and about his suggestions for more acceptable behavior. As the employee tries to change, the manager should give him immediate and useful feedback about the extent to which his efforts to change his behavior meet the manager's standards.

Group development programs conducted by professionals may be even more helpful. Managers should consider team building or organization development programs to assist in improving personal interaction.

[2] See Edgar H. Schein and Warren G. Bennis, *Personal and Organizational Change Through Group Methods: The Laboratory Approach,* John Wiley & Sons, Inc., New York, 1965.

[3] For an excellent method, see "Behavior-DATA" by David W. Merrill, private publication of Personnnel Predictions & Research, Inc., 200 Fillmore Street, Denver, Colorado 80206, 1973.
See also: Fred E. Fiedler, "Style or Circumstance; the Leadership Enigma," *Psychology Today,* March 1969.

[4] John H. Zenger and Dale E. Miller, "Building Effective Teams," *Personnel,* March–April 1974.

chapter 8

The
salary appraisal

TO RECOMMEND OR NOT TO RECOMMEND A SALARY INCREASE
for an employee? On the one hand are the pressures of the
relationship between manager and employee and the need to
reward each person adequately for his contribution; on the
other, the pressures of profit; in the middle, the manager. No
wonder many accept an administrative system that takes the
decision out of their hands or a system of automatic increases
up to some fixed point in the salary scale.

Most companies, however, expect the manager to take
responsibility for pay as for all other matters affecting professional, supervisory, and other management employees. His
actions are, of course, subject to review by others, and he is

expected to live within the salary policies and philosophy of the firm.

The problem for the manager lies in the fact that he is expected to get results, to make certain defined contributions to the business. But he is not expected to do this at all costs. And so his money resources must be as carefully and skillfully handled as other resources. But the key to his achieving needed results is the employee who, by his ingenuity and commitment, produces these results. If he is to give his best, he must feel he is being fairly treated. If the manager is to live up to his own principles, he also has a need to feel that he is treating the employee fairly.

THE IMPACT OF THE MERIT INCREASE

To many employees, once a level of income has been reached that provides for the basic necessities of life, the major impact of the merit increase may be its symbolism.[1] It represents the manager's satisfaction with performance, his recognition of special effort. It says to the employee, "You have done something that is worth more than just words, something a little awkward and a little hard to give, that required a little effort and justification on my part." And since it did require some justification, the employee regards it as special.

The absence of a merit increase at a time when the employee feels it is about due has a reverse effect. It symbolizes some level of dissatisfaction with performance, regardless of the soundness of the explanation that may be given for its absence. And the employee feels a growing insecurity in his relationship with his manager.

The manager, usually also an employee, experiences the same feelings about his personal salary situation in his relationship with his own boss. So he has a more than usual awareness of the employee's reactions, and this may make it even harder to reach an objective decision about salary.

[1] Frederick Herzberg, Bernard Mausner, and Barbara Bloch Snyderman, *The Motivation to Work,* John Wiley & Sons, New York, 1957.

The whole matter is made more difficult because it is not completely possible to measure, in any objective sense, the work of professional, supervisory, and other management employees. And yet the performance of this work is one of the major determinants of salary decisions once a person has been hired. The manager is therefore forced to rely on his judgment for his decision. But his judgment will be sounder if it is based on sufficient representative information about the major relevant factors incorporated in the salary philosophy of his firm.

FACTORS IN MAKING A SALARY APPRAISAL

Each organization must decide what it pays for, and managerial judgments are then focused on this decision. For most, however, salary judgments are based on five general factors: (1) the performance of the employee, (2) a comparison of his pay with that of other employees, (3) the market value of the employee outside the company, (4) the employee's individual situation, and (5) the administrative and business guidelines currently in effect. Let's look at each of these factors in detail.

1. *The employee's performance.* This factor is discussed elsewhere (see Chapters 4, 6, and 10 especially) since it is an ingredient in many types of employee appraisal. Basic here is the need for defining the position so that both manager and employee know what the employee is expected to do, what area of work he is responsible for. In any given period of time, the employee may not work at *all* phases of his responsibility. His

---

Basic Factors in Salary Appraisal

1. Employee's performance.
2. Comparisons of his pay with that of other employees.
3. Employee's market value outside the company.
4. Individual considerations.
5. Current business and administrative guidelines.

specific assignments or goals may in fact represent less than half the total work for which he is accountable.

For example, a man who is hired to improve a business's cost accounting may, in a given year, devise a system, install the necessary procedures, and put a new recording and reporting system into effect in only two of, say, seven departments. And a management development specialist, expected to accumulate employee assessment information, renovate the promotion system, streamline training programs, and evolve assignments of the musical chair type for especially promotable individuals, may have made a frontal attack on data collection and promotion but may still have the other areas to tackle. The salary attached to a position (often expressed in terms of a minimum and a maximum amount based on an evaluation of the position's worth to the business) is, however, usually set on the basis of the *total* job. In evaluating the performance of the employee the manager therefore needs to consider not only the work actually assigned for the period but also the total scope of the position.

Probably the simplest thing for him to do is to list the major day-to-day continuing activities of the employee and, roughly, the percentage of time devoted to them. Then he should itemize special projects assigned during the period together with the approximate time available to work on them and their planned and actual starting and completion dates. Next to each item he should list any agreed-upon standards for successful accomplishment and make brief notes on the status of each work item. What has been accomplished? What still needs to be done? Then he should summarize in each case his evaluation of the employee's progress.

He should make notes of situational factors—that is, any factors outside the employee's control that have made it easier or harder for the employee to work effectively. These include hold-ups in other parts of the organization, unanticipated crash programs, organization or staffing shifts, delays in materials, and lack of adequate resources. He should also list major responsibilities of the position that have not yet been assigned so that they are factored into the judgmental decision.

Having followed this procedure for each item, the manager should be able to sum up what appear to be the employee's most significant accomplishments, identify the areas of his work most in need of attention, and make an overall judgment of the value of his work during the period in question. See Exhibits 1 and 2 at the end of the book.

2. *Comparisons with other employees.* The next phase of salary appraisal involves a look at data about other employees who make a roughly comparable contribution. In many firms, these data are published periodically so that managers may have ready access to them. In smaller companies it may be necessary to discuss the situation with associate managers to determine their salary practices. The fundamental involved is to avoid penalizing the employee because he is working for a tough manager with exceptionally high standards or over-rewarding

---

Data About Other Employees to Be Considered in Salary Appraisal

1. Average salary increase given in the firm during the preceding year.
2. Average salary increase given in the department during the preceding year.
3. Percentage of company employees receiving increases during the preceding year.
4. Percentage of departmental employees receiving increases during the preceding year.
5. Average performance rating of employees in the firm.
6. Average performance rating of employees in the department.
7. Specific salary action taken for employees doing directly comparable work.
8. Specific salary action taken for employees holding the same or a similar title.

him because he is working for a soft manager whose standards, to say the least, are modest. Data of specific interest probably include average salary increases in the company and in the department during the past year, percentage of employees receiving increases, average lapse of time since the last increase, and average performance rating (if overall judgments about performance are summarized in a number or letter rating).

The objective in considering these data is not to treat the employee like all other employees; it is rather to know what the norm is and then deliberately treat him as differently as the manager believes he merits.

In addition, the manager needs to look specifically at the salary treatment of a few employees whose work is either comparable or distinctly different in some known way from that of the employee in question. For example, if the employee is on a training program and his contribution seems about the same as other trainees, the manager should investigate how the salaries of the others are being handled. Or if an employee has the same title as another elsewhere in the organization but the work he is doing is decidedly different, the manager should investigate the salary of the other employee to insure that his treatment of the employee recognizes the difference.

3. *Market value outside the company*. Phase 3 of salary appraisal involves a candid look at what other companies are doing. For some reason, managers often feel there is something wrong about this, that employees should be paid what they are "worth," and that this magic worth is fixed in heaven. Factually, worth in our economy is more often fixed in the marketplace than anywhere else. And it is only common sense to investigate what competitors are doing for employees of comparable responsibility and skill. *Competitor* is used here not in the sense of a business or industry competitor; rather it means any company that may be in competition for the services of the individual whose salary is being reviewed.

Large companies usually survey the market periodically for this kind of information and factor it into their salary structure. Smaller firms rely on management associations and consulting firms to supply such data. The American Management Associations conducts and publishes the findings of such a survey, and the Department of Labor's Bureau of Labor Statistics is also a source of published data. Naturally these surveys focus on positions that are fairly standard throughout industry, and they are subject to the usual discrepancies. For example, what a production manager does in one company may be quite different from what one does in another, so it is important not to be deceived by a job title and to look instead at comparable responsibilities. For unusual positions such as specialized engineering work, recruiting firms or search firms may be of help in identifying the going rate.

Again, the idea in gathering and considering such information is not simply to pay the individual what another firm would pay him. It is to factor into managerial judgment the cost of replacing the employee so that the decision is made in full possession of all the facts and both the risk of losing the employee and fairness with respect to his personal situation are considered. The manager, of course, should recognize that situations will always exist in which a given employee will be worth a great deal more or a great deal less to another company. The intent is therefore to look at comparable situations and not try to outguess the special ones.

4. *The employee's individual situation.* Next the manager needs to turn his attention to the employee as an individual. He should first consider basic statistical information. If the employee's position has a minimum and a maximum salary, where within this range does he stand? Then a look at his salary history is necessary, because probably this history determines his expectations. In the past five years or so, what has his salary treatment been? How frequently has he received increases, in what amounts, and with what average performance rating (if this has been recorded)? What trend or trends have been apparent? Up? Down? Leveling out? Just where is he with respect to the working population? Pretty far down the scale? In a moder-

ate position? Or comfortably well up? Specifically, how long has it been since his last increase? And how much was that increase?

Then some thought must be given to the kind of person he is. Has money been an important motivator in the past? How dependent emotionally does he seem to be upon receiving a raise? The intent here is not to get away with as little as possible but rather to adjust salary action to individual temperament insofar as the manager is able to see it. For example, a pretty

---

A Few Individual Considerations in Salary Appraisal

1. How frequently have increases been given during the past five years?
2. What has been the average size of the employee's increases during the past five years?
3. What performance ratings has he been given (if recorded)?
4. What trends have been established as to frequency of increase?
5. What trends have been established as to size of increase?
6. What trends do the employee's performance ratings show (if recorded)?
7. Are the trends in salary consistent with the trends in performance rating (if recorded)?
8. How does the employee's current salary compare with the established minimum and maximum for the job?
9. How long has he been in this position?
10. What is the relationship between his pay and that of the total working population?
11. What effect have past increases had on his performance (if known)?
12. When was his last increase?
13. How much was his last increase?
14. What is his apparent potential in the company?

insecure individual who equates lack of increase with lack of managerial confidence should perhaps be given somewhat smaller increases somewhat more frequently, whereas another individual who has more confidence in himself is likely to be more satisfied and more productive with larger increases a little further apart. These are gross judgments, of course, and if a manager does not feel he knows the employee's reactions well enough, he may prefer to ignore this factor. But it is important to note that he has two aspects of a possible increase to decide —dollars and timing—and that both can be varied effectively in making salary decisions.

Basically the intent is to decide whether there are some circumstances implicit in these data that may override other factors. What about the employee's apparent potential? Is he moving ahead rapidly? Or is this likely to be a terminal job? Is it so long since the last increase that the manager is virtually compelled to recommend action now or face a feeling of injustice on the part of the employee, a fall-off in his peformance, a strong deterioration in their relationship, a decision to seek another position, or some other unfortunate result?

5. *Administrative and business guidelines.* Probably every company has a salary philosophy or at least some traditional salary practices. For example, there may be written or unwritten rules that in fact limit the size of an increase. The personnel department may regulate the frequency with which the manager reviews salaries. Or the manager's authority to grant increases may be restricted to prescribed amounts or time intervals; and if he exceeds the one or shortens the other, additional approvals may be needed.

Business conditions also affect the granting of increases. If a company is in serious difficulty financially or if a department's costs show an alarming tendency to rise more rapidly than its profits, special limitations on increases as well as other expenditures may go into effect. Or a contract negotiated with union-represented employees may spell out a series of automatic adjustments in pay that will place categories of unorganized lower-level employees in a relatively poor position unless this factor is considered along with merit when recommending salary changes.

The economic inflation of recent years has added to the complexity of decision making in the salary area. Some firms have granted general cost-of-living increases to help keep pace with the rising price of necessities. Others have changed the wage structure, that is, they have increased the minimum and maximum pay assigned to a position so that when a manager reviews the status of a person he does so against increasingly higher pay standards. (This condition has another possible result. If an employee is not contributing as well as a manager believes is required by his position, failure to give him a raise effectively results in a pay cut.)

When there are government regulations on size of salary increases for a firm or an industry or a trade, they place additional constraints on managerial decision making. They often necessitate additional review and input by a third-party salary administrator for the firm or department.

When the manager considers the desirability of salary action, he considers all these opportunities and constraints, not so that he can apply what he learns in blanket fashion, but rather so that he can give it adequate consideration in deciding how a particular employeee should be treated.

Having gathered information on each of the five salary appraisal factors, the manager needs now to review it as a whole, weigh and digest it, and then reach a judgmental decision about what should be done. See Exhibit 4 for a suggested format of the salary appraisal summary.

If he needs to obtain the approval of his boss or the personnel department, he will want to document his information carefully and be prepared to defend his recommendation. He will therefore want to document his reasoning in arriving at his decision. This will be of value to him not only in obtaining the needed approval but also later, if approval is received, in discussing the matter with the employee.

His appraisal decision, of course, may be to *not* grant an increase at a given time. If this is the case, he will especially want to document his reasoning and indicate when the employee's situation should be reviewed again—and what now appears to be the thing he should do to change the decision next time around if it is possible to do so.

The salary appraisal is based on information in five areas: the performance of the employee, a comparison of his pay with the salary treatment of other employees in the firm, his market value outside the company, the employee's individual situation, and whatever administrative and business guidelines are currently in effect. Whether the decision is favorable or not, the information collected and the reason for the decision need to be documented for the manager's immediate use and for future reference.

chapter 9

Salary action

THE MANAGER WHO BEGINS TO PLAN HIS COURSE OF ACTION after making his salary appraisal decision has waited too long.

Oh, yes, he can obtain whatever approvals may be necessary to put salary recommendations into effect. He can complete required forms and notify the pay office. He can even use sound tactics in notifying the employee. But if he really wants his salary action to have a sustained, favorable impact on the employee's attitude, commitment, and performance, he should have begun to communicate months before.

THE FOUR OBJECTIVES

A manager probably has at least four objectives in salary communication:

1. To help the employee understand why his salary is what it is and, to the extent possible, to show that it is fair.
2. To let the employee know where he stands in his present job and what his prospects appear to be on that job and with respect to advancement.
3. To obtain from the employee his thoughtful reaction to his present and prospective work situation so that this information can be factored into the manager's thinking with respect to the employee's development.
4. To strengthen the relationship further so that in the future the employee will be more responsive to the manager's coaching and development efforts and will bring obstacles and barriers to the manager for their joint attention.

None of these can be achieved on a one-shot basis. All are interlocked with many other managerial actions and depend heavily on an effective day-to-day working relationship. How, then, specifically through communication, appraisal, and action on salary matters, can a manager work toward these objectives?

1. *Employee understanding of pay.* The critical thing here is to set up the situation properly in the first place. Don't wait until salary action is taken or is about to be taken before discussing current ground rules. In most cases feelings of disappointment, dissatisfaction, and unfairness are aroused in an employee because his personal experience, the shared experiences of other employees, his guess about what is being done generally, or his lack of knowledge about what is being done and his consequent hope or dream about what will be done make him expect more than he receives or expect action sooner.

In an effort to avoid such misunderstanding, the manager should, throughout the year, discuss both the firm's salary philosophy and practices and his own practices—how often he reviews salaries, his personal ground rules for amount of increase, what percentages represent modest, good, and substantial increases, and so on.

Next, any consolidated data with respect to average amount and frequency of increases in the company or department should be made known. Employees try to determine these figures for themselves on the basis of whatever information they are able to glean from one another, and it is usually sounder for them to have factual rather than imaginary data. In addition, any conditions, either internal or external, that may limit the manager's decision should be brought out into the open. For example, if business is poor, if costs are rising out of proportion to prices, the manager may need to delay increases longer than usual or make them smaller than usual. He will do well to make this known to employees as soon as he recognizes the fact himself.

So far the suggested information is entirely general. It says in effect, "This is how our salary system works around here and why, and this is the impact on employees generally." Now with respect to the individual: If the job has been evaluated and assigned a minimum and a maximum salary and a grade of some kind, the manager should, at the time the employee accepts the position, let him know his job grade and salary range for the work. At a later time the grade should probably be

---

Salary Information for Employee

General:
1. Company's salary philosophy, plan, and practices.
2. Manager's personal salary practices.
3. Average amount and frequency of employee increases.
4. Any limiting business conditions.

Specific:
1. Job grade, if established.
2. Minimum and maximum for the job, if existing.
3. Specific ground rules for earning an increase.
4. Employee's job responsibilities.
5. Work results expected of the employee.
6. Measures, criteria, standards, or ground rules for success.

reaffirmed since its importance may not be clear to the employee at the time he begins a new job and he may forget it. In addition, the manager's own criteria with respect to earning an increase should be communicated to the employee so that he is in full possession of the rules of the game.

Finally the manager needs to be attentive to his responsibilities toward the employee, particularly as they concern the delegation of work. The employee's duties should be discussed thoroughly and should preferably be reduced to writing in a brief, clear job statement. In addition, as each assignment is made, the manager needs to be certain that both are in agreement about the result the employee is expected to achieve and any ground rules for achieving it. Then, as the work is done, the manager needs to be certain that the employee is aware of the extent to which he has succeeded as well as his manager's view of his performance in achieving results. If the manager uses a work planning and progress review method of delegating, he can probably assume with some confidence that the employee does indeed know his manager's feelings about performance and, hopefully, shares them.

If all these things are done well in advance of salary review, the odds are that the employee will not expect action that is considerably out of line with the manager's decision. Then when it comes to the point of discussing the specific salary decision, the manager usually has only to tell the employee and describe his reasons rather simply. This does not imply that the employee is always happy and satisfied with his pay—but he is more likely to understand and accept the manager's decision.

2. *Employee knowledge of where he stands.* There seems to be an almost universal need for an employee to know how highly he is valued in his present position and in terms of the future. If the manager has held frequent discussions about the employee's work, this should be pretty well understood, at least implicitly. But in addition there needs to be periodic confirmation or reassurance that the employee's interpretation of the manager's actions and attitude toward him has been

correct. If a salary increase is given, this, of course, sums up the manager's evaluation of the employee's current worth, particularly if it is accompanied by a few carefully selected words. If no increase is given and nothing is said about it, the employee's insecurity tends to grow until the situation is brought out into the open and discussed frankly.

Respect for the employee as a human being demands discussion with him of the reasons for his being passed over, particularly if it has happened more than once. Even an experienced employee, one whose work is excellent and whose pay is therefore at or close to the maximum, needs the reassurance of a word from his manager that the lack of a pay increase is because he is already well paid within the range believed right for his work. He deserves as well the opportunity to discuss his prospects for upward re-evaluation of his current work through the addition of related responsibilities or favorable consideration for promotion. And certainly the employee whose work simply does not merit an increase in pay deserves the opportunity to discuss what he needs to do to change that decision at the next review.

These are not matters about which the manager should be "kind." The more thoughtful, the more perceptive, the more aware the manager is, the more realistic and factual he needs to be—and will want and try to be—since only in this way can the employee make a realistic evaluation of his total situation. And only if he is able to do this is he really free to make the kind of choice—to stay or leave—that permits full commitment of his personal resources of talent and energy to accomplishing the work for which he is responsible.

3. *Employee reaction to his salary progress.* Although the employee is not expected to testify against himself on the job any more than in a court of law, salary discussion time is usually a good occasion for the manager to lay the basis for *later* exploration of development needs and career interests.

The employee who has been given an increase usually experiences a surge of warm feeling toward his boss. Even though notification time is *not* right for lengthy exploration of performance improvement and career development, the suggestion that these be discussed within a relatively short period is usually welcomed. So when the manager notifies the employee of a salary increase, he may well set the date for this kind of discussion. If the employee is not fully on top of his job, the manager may suggest that the employee prepare for the discussion by reviewing how he thinks he is doing and what performance areas he feels he needs most to improve, together with any suggestions he may have of ways to improve or ways in which his manager can be of help. See Exhibits 1 and 2. The manager may want to prepare a coaching appraisal as in Exhibit 3. For the employee who is on top of his job, a look at career interests will probably be appropriate. The format outlined in Exhibit 7 may serve as a preparation guide for both individuals.

The employee who has not been given an increase will, of course, have had a somewhat fuller discussion of the reasons for the manager's action. He may have questioned the manager at some length and may have expressed his disappointment, cited reasons for his failure to perform as expected, and argued against the manager's reasoning. The manager will need to be a sympathetic, patient, and responsive listener. If the employee presents new evidence not previously considered, the manager may wish to add it to his salary appraisal information and, following the meeting, rethink his decision to be sure that it still seems wise. In any case, having heard the employee out, the manager may bring the discussion to a close profitably by suggesting that it is important for the same deficiencies in communication and performance not to recur. He then sets a meeting date, perhaps two or three weeks later, to focus on ways of accomplishing needed results in the areas of deficiency. (See Chapter 5 for suggestions on this subject.) Given time to adjust to the situation, the employee who has been penalized for performance deficiencies may well be more than usually ready to set new learning goals for himself and therefore responsive to the manager's coaching.

4. *Stronger employee-manager relationship.* The very fact that the manager discusses the reasons for his salary decision and listens with some care and attention to the employee's reaction will clarify the relationship between the two. It may or may not strengthen it. Whether it does depends to a large extent on the relationship built on the foundation of day-by-day communication (both word and action) between them. If the discussions following a salary decision support the already existing relationship, then it will endure and it may be strengthened. However, if the discussions do not support the relationship, it is very likely that the two parties will later revert to the old pattern, and any special effect of the salary discussion will be temporary. Chapter 3 explores the relationship problem in detail, but a fundamental principle holding here is that the manager cannot expect to create a favorable relationship on a one- or even a two-shot basis. The groundwork for a sound working relationship needs to be laid long before salary appraisal.

If that relationship is adequate, then careful decision making with respect to salary—adequately explained and followed by an open-minded hearing of the employee's comments and a workmanlike exploration of ways and means of helping him overcome performance deficiencies or prepare himself for more responsibility—will contribute to its continuing soundness. If the relationship is poor, the same process may enable manager and employee to make a start toward improving it, but the more favorable atmosphere will then need to be sustained in the way they work together from that point forward.

SO WHAT?

To summarize what is required for effective salary action: The manager needs first to lay the proper groundwork with each employee prior to making his salary appraisal. Following his decision, he needs, second, to hold at least two carefully planned salary discussions—one for notification purposes and one to consider the "so what?" problem; that is, to translate the salary decision into meaningful things both employee and manager can do to sustain, improve, or change such decisions in the future.

Notification should be done in private, preferably in person, and briefly. The manager should tell the employee the decision he has made and his reasons for it. It is easy to err by saying too little or too much, or by saying it at the wrong time. The manager, for example, who simply tells the employee that he will receive a certain increase on a certain date, or, worse still, notifies him in writing and lets it go at that, misses an obvious opportunity to strengthen their relationship.

The manager, on the other hand, who seizes the opportunity to help improve the employee's performance by entering into a long and detailed discussion either before or after he mentions an increase is usually wasting his breath. Employees sense the approach of the salary subject and only half-mindedly hear and respond to the discourse. And once the amount has been mentioned, they manipulate it arithmetically, ponder several choices for spending it, and so on.

A few carefully chosen words are best. The manager should let the employee know quickly what the situation is and sum up the company's feeling about him and his work. If an increase is given, for example, the manager could say something like this: "Mary, I'm very pleased to tell you that beginning on such and such a date your salary will be increased to $XX per month. Your work has been excellent [or coming along well] during the past year, and you deserve this increase." After the employee has responded, the manager could go on to say, "I think it would be a good idea for us to get together in the next couple of weeks to talk a little about your future. If you agree, let's set a date right now." After the date is set, the manager may indicate anything that needs to be done to prepare for the discussion.

If an increase is not given, the manager might say quite simply: "Mary, I've reviewed your work and salary situation and decided that an increase is not justified right now. These are my reasons." He would then give her the major determining factors that led to his decision. After Mary has had a chance to ask questions and argue and the whole matter has been thoroughly discussed, the manager could say, "I know you're disappointed, Mary, so let's get together soon to take a hard look at what we can each do to help see that this situation doesn't occur next time around." With the date set, all that remains is to indicate anything Mary needs to do to prepare herself for the discussion.

If the employee's work is excellent but an increase has not been given because her pay is already close to the maximum permitted, the manager can say: "Mary, I've just been looking at your work and salary situation. I'm sure you know I feel your work is excellent. I'm sure you also know that you're being paid pretty close to maximum. Now, the maximum figure still seems to us to be about right for your kind of work. I would like, though, to get together with you and see how you feel about what you're doing and about your future with us. So if you'd like to do this too, let's set a date."

For an employee close to retirement, this approach could be used: "Mary, I've been taking a look at your work and salary situation, and I think you know how much we appreciate your contribution to our company over the years. It seems to us your pay is about right as it is, but I'd like to get together with you to be sure that you're getting satisfaction from your work, that you're preparing yourself for retirement in a year or so, and that we're capitalizing on all your years of experience. If you'd like to talk about these things too, let's set a date."

When both parties have prepared themselves appropriately, the "so what?" discussion takes place. It may take the form of a performance improvement planning session for the employee whose major efforts should be channeled into her present job, a career development discussion for the employee who is on top of her job and seems promotable, a termination discussion for the failing employee, or, for the retiring employee, a goal-setting session in which she and her manager pinpoint a few things the employee can do prior to her retirement to leave in available form at least some of her wealth of usable, accumulated experience.

Having made his appraisal of an employee's salary situation, reached a decision, and obtained whatever approvals may be required, the manager needs to discuss his decision with the employee and later work with him on performance improvement or career planning. Salary action is likely to increase the employee's commitment to achieve needed work results and to strengthen the working relationship between the two only if it has been preceded by effective communication about work responsibilities and current performance accomplishments as well as the manager's salary philosophy, practices, and current administrative ground rules so that the employee's expectations are realistic.

chapter 10

Termination
appraisal and action

OCCASIONALLY A MANAGER REACHES THE POINT OF ADMITTING
to himself that a given employee is not producing. This is
seldom a single or sudden appraisal. Rather it evolves over a
period of time through a variety of incidents.

At one point the manager may become aware that some
important piece of work is behind schedule; at another, that a
customer is complaining about inadequate service; at yet
another, that the employee is not handling a situation as well as
he should. Finally some incident or episode triggers full awareness that overall the employee's work is not satisfactory.
Perhaps the manager has just reviewed the employee's salary
and realized that he cannot recommend an increase, or perhaps

his own manager's questions about development plans make him realize that the employee is at best operating at minimum levels. In any event, having reached his conclusion, he needs to take direct and immediate action to remedy the situation.

The action he takes should strive for two results: rapid improvement in work that is lagging behind schedule and, equally important, preservation of the employee's self-confidence and self-respect. Neither is easy to accomplish. The former requires incisive analysis of the employee's performance problems and innovative, constructive suggestions for improvement. The latter requires an open-minded, supportive attitude that permits dealing with the employee with absolute fairness, with attention to objective fact, and with a clearly displayed awareness of the employee's personal value and areas of performance strength.

The assumption is made in this chapter that the employee may be treated as an individual—that he is not a member of an organized group that must be dealt with according to a prescribed set of regulations covered in a written contract. Also excluded from consideration are problems of seniority, tenure, and the like, which depend on the philosophy and practices of the individual firm.

Looking, then, only at the appraisal problem and the subsequent action planning, we suggest the following as a reasonable approach.

1. Make a formal appraisal of the employee's work and document it. (Exhibit 1.)
2. Communicate the appraisal conclusions to the employee.
3. Determine the reasons for poor performance and make constructive suggestions for improvement.
4. Establish a probationary period and develop plans for the work to be accomplished during it.
5. Provide adequate coaching and support during the probationary period.
6. Summarize and document the appraisal of performance during the probationary period.

7. Communicate the final decision to the employee and establish ground rules for the future.

MAKE A FORMAL APPRAISAL AND DOCUMENT IT

The manager's awareness of the employee's marginal performance represents an informal appraisal. It may well be based on a look at only a few parts of the employee's job. Its supporting evidence may be vague and fuzzy. Before reaching such an important decision, the manager needs to make a thorough review of all the employee's important responsibilities, what he has and has not accomplished against them, and what overall appear to be his major performance strengths and deficiencies.

One of the easiest ways to do this is to list the assignments given the employee in the past six months, make notes next to each item on what the employee did and did not accomplish, then estimate whether the accomplishments were up to standard and, if not, why not. Exhibit 1 is a reasonable format for doing this. If the manager is using a work-planning and progress-review approach as described in Chapter 6, much of this information will already be available and the employee may, in fact, be completely aware of his failure to achieve established goals.

COMMUNICATE APPRAISAL CONCLUSIONS TO THE EMPLOYEE

If the manager still concludes that, having documented his appraisal in a systematic fashion, the work has not been satisfactory, he needs to plan his communication of that fact to the employee. This communication must of course be adapted to the individual employee and to the kind of relationship that has existed between the two parties, but a few ground rules are worth keeping in mind.

Take early action. Sometimes managers dread taking the necessary action and postpone communicating with the employee so long that the time given him to shape up is inadequate. Unless his poor performance involves very simple problems of the self-discipline type, such as tardiness or absenteeism, the employee needs turn-around time—usually about two to three months. This becomes a probationary time, then, in which he may not only try harder but also study or work with someone who may be able to help him improve a knowledge or skill area.

Be straightforward. Since the manager has concluded that the employee's performance has been unsatisfactory, and since this decision is not subject to negotiation, problem solving, or other give-and-take discussion, it is probably wisest for the manager to be straightforward and direct in telling the employee his conclusion and the reasons for it. He should, of course, be willing to listen to explanations, justifications, and rationalizations. He should be willing to modify his conclusions if significant new information comes to light. But on the whole, it is the manager's responsibility in this situation to level with the employee so that he can base his self-appraisal and subsequent action planning on a true picture of the manager's judgment. Tact is good, but being specific and clear is even more important in this discussion.

Don't be in a hurry. This is a difficult time for both manager and employee. Although neither enjoys the discussion, the manager owes it to the employee to be willing to explore matters thoroughly, answer questions, give examples, perhaps even admit to some personal weaknesses. The employee needs to feel satisfied that he understands fully what is in the manager's mind even though he may not agree with it. The manager does not need to feel guilty because he cannot perfectly measure the employee's performance. It would be nice if this could be done, but it is usually not possible with today's management tools.

Let the employee talk if he wants to. After the manager has explained how he feels about the employee's performance, the employee may react somewhat emotionally. He may deny the manager is right, try to explain himself, or blame others. The manager should be prepared for this reaction and should listen to a reasonable amount of it in order to let the employee air to his boss, rather than to his associates, any feelings of injustice he may have. If possible, he should help guide the employee from such negative thoughts toward a more constructive frame of mind. In particular, realizing the nature of the reaction and the feelings of disappointment, hurt, and guilt that have generated it, he should not add to the negative climate by an emotional reaction of his own. This is not the time for him to be angry, sarcastic, or derogatory. He may need to set the record straight on certain issues, but he should choose a time when the employee is in a mood to listen.

Reactions will vary considerably among employees, of course. In some instances, a person may need encouragement to say what is in his mind. In others, the reaction may be an explosion. The important thing is that the manager be alert to signals that the employee wants to talk out his feelings and, if these appear, let him.

Plan on several sessions if necessary. If the past working relationship has been one marked by frequent review of accomplishment and adjustment of plans, there may be no need for several discussion sessions, but the manager should be prepared for them. A good rule of thumb is that it is better to schedule several periods of an hour to an hour and a half than to try to get everything done in one long four- or five-hour interview. Long sessions are a strain on both parties. Both get tired. Both get defensive. It is better for them to have some adjustment time so that new thoughts can enter the picture, defensive reactions can disappear, and a more logical "What shall we do about it?" approach becomes possible.

DETERMINE REASONS FOR INADEQUATE PERFORMANCE AND MAKE CONSTRUCTIVE SUGGESTIONS

When the manager's judgments and the reasons for them have been made clear, and when the employee's first reaction is past and he is able to examine his work with some degree of coherence, manager and employee need to think through the areas of poor performance with some care and consider their improvement as a joint task.

On the employee's side there are undoubtedly knowledge and skill areas that need upgrading, performance habits and personal attitudes that need change. On the manager's side there are undoubtedly clarifications of assigned work and standards, improvement in level of communication, and possible changes in paperwork, work methods, organization, and so on that can be effected. These all need to be identified, after which agreement must be reached about desirable actions each man will take and their timing. Exhibits 1 and 3 will serve as a reasonable format.

ESTABLISH PROBATIONARY PERIOD AND WORK PLANS

Finally, the manager needs to establish the period during which the employee will be given an opportunity to improve his performance, specify appropriate work goals, and set the standards or ground rules for accomplishing them. Also needed is the employee's agreement to work toward these goals and to meet these standards.

This is the point at which the manager who wishes to be fair should leave nothing to chance. His goal is to be sure that the employee understands what is expected of him and what is at stake if he is unsuccessful. A good way of being sure is to ask the employee to write down his understanding of the situation for the manager's review. This has some advantages, but it may require another meeting if what the employee writes does not agree with the manager's understanding.

Some managers write the employee a note confirming their discussions. This may clarify the record, but since it is difficult to write both clearly and tactfully, the effect may be to arouse negative feelings again. A possible compromise is to develop the written statement together and then make sure each side has a copy. This takes longer but may be soundest in the end. The material provides data for parts of Exhibit 1 if this format is used to document accomplishment during the probationary period.

PROVIDE ADEQUATE COACHING AND SUPPORT

This is a period of almost constant appraisal on the part of both manager and employee. Because the employee is being given more critical attention than usual, insecurity and uneasiness are generated, which may make sound working relationships difficult. On the other hand, knowing he has upset the employee and perhaps suffering some guilt feelings of his own, the manager often tends to avoid the employee. He may even rationalize his actions as "giving him a chance" to improve. A few resolutions during this period are in order for him.

Determine to end the probationary period with increased respect. Allow the employee every opportunity to improve his performance—set specific goals for him; clarify the way in which his success will be measured; give him rapid, useful, frequent feedback; listen to his comments on problems and obstacles more carefully than usual. All this will help the manager to arrive at a clear-cut decision as to whether the employee has improved enough to be kept on the job. A "perhaps" or "maybe" decision at the end of the probationary period implies such a lack of confidence in both employee and manager that it is doubtful whether an effective working relationship between the two is possible. This dilemma can be avoided by setting realistic, measurable goals in the first place so that, at the end of the period, there is no question in either person's mind about the outcome.

Plan increased contacts during the probationary period. The manager who has told an employee that he is not satisfied with his performance cannot help being aware of the uneasy relationship between them. Under the circumstances his reaction may again be to avoid the employee once he has been put on notice. In order to be fair as well as to observe changes in performance behavior and in results, the manager needs instead to increase the frequency of his contacts—not so that the employee feels he is breathing down his neck but so that he feels support, interest, a willingness to share required business information, and the availability of help if needed. The contacts should also be occasions for feedback so that throughout the period the employee knows exactly where he stands and the eventual decision, pro or con, comes as no surprise.

Document performance more thoroughly than usual during the probationary period. The entire probationary period is

---

A Few Ground Rules for Managers During the Probation Period

1. Take action early enough to give the employee a fair chance to improve.

2. Be straightforward and explicit about improvement needs so that the employee understands what is expected of him.

3. Allow enough time for discussion so that the employee has the opportunity to explore his total work situation thoroughly.

4. Let the employee discuss work problems fully so that any grievances are aired and off his chest.

5. Plan to take several shorter sessions (rather than one long one) to cover appraisal, work problems, goal setting for the probationary period, and so on. This allows for adjustment to the situation on both sides.

6. Determine to end the probationary period with increased respect.

7. Plan increased contacts during the probationary period to keep the communication level high and to permit useful, rapid feedback to the employee.

8. Document performance more thoroughly than usual during the probationary period so that there is adequate information for final decision making.

9. Emphasize the employee's personal and performance strengths during the appraisal and feedback sessions so that he can build on these.

one of appraisal—and critical appraisal at that. The manager's documentation of all pertinent information about the employee's performance, behavior, relationships, methods, and results is the basis for his later judgment, and he will want this most serious judgment to be based on evidence that is as factual, objective, and representative as possible. Notes should therefore be more thorough than usual and should adhere closely to the goals set for the probationary period. Exhibit 1 may be used for such notes, shortening time intervals appropriately.

Emphasize strengths in appraisal and feedback. Since this is a period of scrutiny which could end in termination, there is a tendency for the manager to emphasize failures in performance and discrepancies between accomplishment and pre-established standards. He can, in fact, so undermine his employee's confidence in a situation that is already hazardous that it may have the effect of making the unfortunate employee less capable than ever of producing results. The manager should therefore be careful to note both specific instances of satisfactory accomplishment and any performance strengths he observes. This is important, too, for the post-probationary period. If the employee remains, both will need to use these strengths as the foundation on which to build continued progress and improvement. If the employee leaves, the information will be vital to him in looking for another job.

SUMMARIZE AND DOCUMENT
APPRAISAL OF PERFORMANCE

Summarizing and documenting the performance appraisal should be relatively easy. If clear, specific, measurable work goals were set at the beginning of the probationary period, if work plans have been developed and mutual agreement reached on them, if the manager has been in close contact with the employee throughout and has been giving him the necessary feedback, this step merely represents the consolidation of all this information. The manager needs to put it in writing, weigh the pros and cons of asking the employee to remain, and finally, make his decision on the best course of action. (Exhibit 1 again provides a possible format.) He needs, too, to make plans for handling the ensuing period if the employee is to stay, since these will have to be discussed promptly.

COMMUNICATE THE FINAL DECISION
TO THE EMPLOYEE

If the final decision calls for the employee to remain on the job, schedule a time to see him and then tell him the decision at once rather than keep him in suspense for an hour while reviewing his performance. Set another time, if possible, to go over his performance during the probationary period in a detailed way and to agree on targets and ground rules for the future. From this point forward the situation becomes one of standard coaching to obtain improved performance, and the standard methods apply even though the employee may need greater than usual reinforcement—that is, encouragement and reassurance—for a while.

If the final decision means the employee must leave, schedule a time to see him, tell him the decision, and explain briefly the reason for it. Too much detail at this point is agonizing for the employee and, if the probationary period was well handled, unnecessary. Instead, place the emphasis on other work he might do successfully, the help that may be available to him from the employment office or elsewhere as an aid to relocation or reassignment, the length of time before his final day, the possibility of taking time off to look for another position, any specific assignments to be completed before the employee leaves, and so on. In other words, focus on the ground rules to be followed during the termination period. The manager should, of course, be prepared to answer questions, listen to the employee's side of the picture, and go into more detail about his performance; but he should firmly but gently move the employee's attention from the past toward the solution of the new problem now facing him—reassignment or change in employer.

THE SEVEN STEPS APPLIED

Let's take an example of the whole termination appraisal process. Manager X, who heads the manufacturing organization, has for some time been concerned about the performance of Peter Brown. Pete is a manufacturing engineer, a graduate of a reputable engineering college with about seven years' experience in design and production engineering, and he has been in his current position for about eight months.

During this time he has had several projects involving changes in manufacturing processes that, it was hoped, would improve product quality and cut manufacturing costs. He has served as a member of a planning team—together with a design engineer, a marketing man, and a cost accountant—working on the introduction of a new product model. In this capacity, he has been asked to report to his team associates on a number of items. He is also expected to help in the shop when emergencies arise on the line and to contribute solutions to problems causing such emergencies.

Manager X has received a complaint from the chairman of the planning team that Pete is not contributing to the effort. He frequently misses meetings or arrives late, and he is often unprepared, even when he has agreed to do a specific piece of work for the team. He gives as his excuse that there have been holdups in the line that required his immediate attention and presence. The complaint increases the manager's awareness that Pete also is seriously late with reports on his projects to improve manufacturing processes.

The manager makes a formal appraisal and documents it. The manager's appraisal documentation shows the way Pete's work can be recorded, following roughly the pattern of Exhibits 1 and 3. Because it itemizes his assignments and his progress toward completing each one, it provides a means of

Basic Record of Performance Appraisal Documentation

PART A

Continuing Responsibilities	Budgets and Standards	Actual Performance During Past Year
1. Troubleshooting in shop.	No line shutdown because of engineering deficiencies.	Superintendent pleased with Pete's help. Has prevented two line stoppages by coming up with quick fixes of a mechanical design nature and has gotten design engineering organization to agree to modifications that make product easier to assemble. Has solved quality problem A through design change and gotten agreement of all parties concerned.
2. Product-planning team.	Attends 100% of meetings. Report ready on assigned projects at each meeting.	Has failed to report on assigned items. Has missed meetings, been late, come unprepared.
3. (Etc.)		

PART B

Major Goals, Involving Programs & Projects	Man-hours	Person Responsible	Begin Date Est.	Begin Date Act.	End Date Est.	End Date Act.	Notes and Comments
Project #1	300	P. Brown	2-1	2-1	5-1	7-1	Analysis of problem sound. Recommendation carefully sold to all involved. Design changes released to drafting room and equipment built and installed. Now functioning satisfactorily.
Project #2	400	P. Brown	2-1	4-15	7-1	?	Investigation under way but no proposals made yet. Shop superintendent waiting for Pete's work on this project. No apparent effort at communication with those depending on results of work. Has not asked for help. Shop pressure for his services has been high.
Project #3				(Etc.)			

ready reference. It shows, for example, that Pete's technical and personal contact competence are good. He appears to be unable to manage his time and lets one phase of his job absorb all his energies. There is no evidence of lack of effort. He just seems unable to juggle several kinds of work at the same time.

Having made this appraisal, the manager checks with another supervisor for whom Pete used to work to see if similar problems have occurred before. They have not, but it is evident that he has not had to handle a situation of quite this kind before.

The manager communicates his appraisal to Pete. Manager X calls Pete, tells him he would like to discuss his work with him, and sets a time. When Pete arrives, Manager X says in a quiet, matter-of-fact tone that a review of his work has led to some conclusions that are not completely favorable. This warns Pete of the general nature of the discussion so that he can be prepared.

Manager X then reviews the status of each phase of Pete's work and his evaluation of where it stands. He lets Pete know that he realizes the problems involved in doing a job that includes a great deal of pressure in some areas and longer-term responsibilities in others, but he points out that this *is* the job and that it needs to be accomplished in total. He then invites Pete to discuss the problems and obstacles he has faced and to explain why some phases of his work have been less than satisfactory.

It becomes apparent as Pete talks that he has become so involved in shop pressures that he just cannot get around to the longer-term projects. He sees their importance but is already sacrificing his personal time to bail the shop out of trouble.

The manager suggests that most jobs have more work in them than can reasonably be accomplished and that the important thing is to allocate time according to priorities and stick to the allocation. He suggests that Pete think the matter over and concentrate on insuring long-term project accomplishment as well as needed shop support. Then they arrange for a second discussion in a few days.

The manager explores Pete's reasons for poor performance and makes constructive suggestions for improvement. At the next meeting, it is apparent that Pete cannot see how to do both kinds of work. When the shifts start up, things are most likely to go wrong in the shop—at 7:00 A.M. and 3:30 P.M. And once he is out on the factory floor, he becomes involved and just doesn't get away.

Manager X makes a few suggestions. He recommends that Pete set aside a certain time of day to work on long-term projects; that these projects be undertaken one at a time rather than several at once; and that Pete prepare a careful, written plan of just what he will do to complete each project successfully. He suggests that Pete talk to the shop superintendent in order to set project priorities and also to work out his allocation of time for troubleshooting. When Pete has done these things, they will get together again to review his work plans. Meanwhile, Manager X will discuss with the manufacturing manager the general problem of engineering support to the factory in an effort to reach understanding and agreement at a higher level in the organization.

The probationary period is established and a work plan is developed. At their third meeting, the manager reviews Pete's time allocation and agrees to it. He reviews Pete's work goals, their priority, and the plans to meet them. Some modifications are made. The manager affirms his confidence in Pete's technical and contact abilities, points out his feeling that the problem is one of managing time, and makes it clear that the next three months will be a testing period to see if Pete can master the problem and remain in his present position. He also makes it clear that he expects the plans to be carried out as agreed; otherwise both men will need to face up to the fact that this is not a suitable position for Pete. Their plan looks about like this:

TIME
ALLOCATION

30%   Goal 1: Complete Project 2 to specification by
                   July 31.
                   a. Complete investigation of sources'
                      high cost by May 20.
                   b. Determine areas for component re-
                      design by May 31.
                   c. Determine areas for materials im-
                      provements by May 31.
                   d. Work with purchasing to identify al-
                      ternate vendors by June 20.
                   e. Perform redesign as required and
                      pilot test by July 1.
                   f. Introduce into factory by July 15.
                   g. Evaluate improvements in cost and
                      performance by July 31.
50%   Goal 2: Continue factory troubleshooting to
                   satisfaction of superintendent.
20%   Goal 3: Contribute to product planning team as
                   requested. (Specify assignments as
                   made with expected completion dates.)

Before Pete leaves, they agree on when they will next meet to
see how things are going.

   *Adequate coaching and support are provided during the
probationary period.* In the interim the manager goes out of his
way to keep in touch with Pete, to talk to him informally, to have
lunch with him. He is careful to transmit quickly any information that might affect Pete's work.

   The first time they review Pete's total progress, Project 2
seems to be coming along well, but it is at the expense of almost
all shop support. Contribution to the product-planning team has
also improved. But it is apparent that Pete has simply with-
drawn from the shop, seated himself at his desk, and gone to
work on delinquent areas. The manager points out again the
necessity for balance in the work and reminds Pete of agreed-
upon time allocations. Pete agrees he must try to handle both.

Coaching Appraisal Summary

1. *What areas of employee's work are going well?* Troubleshooting has been well done. Excellent contribution personally and technically. Relationships good with all concerned. Quality of work on Project #1 high.

2. *What areas of employee's work need strengthening during the next six to twelve months?* Contribution to product-planning team unsatisfactory; fails to attend meetings and reports are late or inadequate. Projects are running late. Planning is inadequate. Work is sporadic on projects.

3. *What future events outside the employee's control may affect, positively or negatively, the employee's ability to accomplish planned results during the next six to twelve months?* Pressure from shop has been high. This will continue for foreseeable future.

4. *What significant strengths has employee demonstrated on this or previous jobs that should be fully used during the next six to twelve months?* He has shown both sound technical competence and good relationships when handling one thing at a time.

5. *What significant gaps in knowledge or experience, what skill development needs or behavior modifications appear desirable for the employee to improve his work during the next six to twelve months?* (Limit to a very few high-priority items, not more than two or three.) He cannot seem to manage his time in the face of extraordinary demands on it. Lets projects suffer to take care of emergencies. Cannot find the balance.

Based on consideration of the above items, summarize coaching decisions:

A. *Manager will do the following (indicate timing):* Talk to Pete. Help with planning and time allocation. (Within one week.)

B. *Manager will recommend that the employee take the following actions (indicate timing):* Set aside time for project work and prepare a written project plan. (Within one week.)

C. *Date for manager to check progress or reevaluate coaching needs:* Two weeks from first meeting.

The manager continues to see Pete frequently after this review and encourages him toward a more balanced effort.

At the subsequent review sessions, however, it becomes more and more apparent that Pete can do the troubleshooting or the project work, but not both. Pete, of course, feels the job is impossible as it is set up, but he is at least aware that he is not meeting the manager's standards with respect to time allocation and balanced effort.

The manager summarizes and documents his appraisal of Pete's performance during this period. Toward the end of the probationary period the manager lists each of the goals agreed to at the beginning of the period and summarizes Pete's efforts toward each. On this basis he reaches the decision that it will be better for all concerned if Pete leaves his position. In brief, his appraisal of Pete's work looks like this:

Goal 1

Phases A, B, and C on schedule. Remaining items incomplete.

Does this work well if relieved of pressure of factory troubleshooting.

GOAL 2

Superintendent satisfied with performance on this point. Continued to develop good solutions to factory problems. Relationships good.

Does this work well but becomes totally absorbed in it to exclusion of other work.

GOAL 3

Work sporadic throughout period of probation. Requested contributions not made.

Ability there, but employee cannot manage his time.

Situational Factors: Pressure from shop was lightened during this period by agreement with superintendent.

Conclusions: Employee is talented and hard-working. He is able to do either engineering work or factory troubleshooting, but not both. This job is a misplacement for him.

The final decision is communicated to Pete, and ground rules are established for the termination period. At the final review session Manager X tells Pete his decision. Pete is unhappy about it, but the decision is expected and he understands the basis for it. Manager X then tries to turn Pete's attention to the performance areas of his greatest strengths—those on which he should base his efforts to find another position. The manager says Pete has a future in straight design engineering that involves only one kind of work at a time. He points out that in view of Pete's good work before he took this job, he is eligible for transfer to another position in the company. Further, the manager indicates the help he will personally give Pete as well as other resources available through the personnel department. He suggests they both investigate the likelihood of a transfer and get together in a few days to discuss how they should handle the next period of time.

At this meeting, having evaluated the employment situation, Manager X sets the termination date, indicates the time off he feels is reasonable for Pete to take for finding other work, and outlines the procedure to follow in requesting a transfer. They agree on what Pete will try to accomplish before he leaves. Manager X reaffirms the help he will give and explains just what he will say about Pete's performance if asked by prospective employers.

The situation is not happy for either Pete or Manager X, but it is a clear-cut one that permits both to function intelligently. The essential human dignity of each is preserved. There is no suggestion that Pete is worthless or that because he has failed on this job he is not suited for any other. Manager X has given him a realistic opportunity, and reasonable help, to improve his performance. In so doing, he has met his responsibilities to Pete. Since Pete has not been able to meet standards, Manager X has taken action to meet his responsibilities to the company—that is, to produce the results he has committed his organization to obtain.

A termination situation is really a series of appraisals of an employee's work based on evaluation of his progress toward agreed-upon results. Having recognized the marginal quality of an employee's performance, the manager documents his findings, communicates them to the employee, and sets a probationary period during which specific work goals are to be accomplished. Throughout the probationary period the manager coaches the employee and reviews his work frequently in an effort to help him overcome performance deficiencies. On the basis of subsequent achievement, the manager decides whether the employee should remain or leave the position and determines the action he should take to implement his decision.

chapter 11

Appraising potential

MOST PRESIDENTS, ESPECIALLY THOSE OF GROWTH companies, are concerned with bringing along today's promising young people as a source of tomorrow's management leadership. Their concern frequently takes the form of translating the company's desired growth into probable numbers and broad qualifications of new managers that will be needed and when. This is usually followed by requests for information regarding staff turnover, retirements, and other details. Once the pertinent information has been assembled, managers down the line are asked to produce runner-up charts, lists of most promising employees, and recommendations of individuals most likely to advance.

There is no doubt about the importance of the problem. It is not necessary that every future manager in a company be home grown; indeed, a strong case can be made for bringing new blood into an organization from time to time. Nevertheless from the firm's point of view some continuity is desirable; and from the capable employee's point of view, opportunity for advancement is a major factor in attracting him originally, holding him, and encouraging his productivity.

In addition to the requests that come down from the top, the manager is also faced with related questions from his employees. From time to time, one of them will ask to talk about his future. "If I stay here, I'd like to have some idea of what my chances for advancement are." Or "Where do you think I might go from here?"

Both questions—"Who is most likely to have what it takes to get ahead?" and "Where can I go from here?"—put the manager on the spot. He has to respond and would actually like to be helpful. In fact, however, the questions are unanswerable with any degree of certainty. What the future will be like for the company ten years hence, what jobs will be open and when, and what requirements will be placed on those who fill them are unknown. On the other hand, what the employee will be like, what knowledge and skill he will have acquired, what his values, motivation, and commitment will be are also unknown. And so the manager must make some judgmental decisions. He must make some predictions about the future.

Faced with this predicament, some managers seem to approach it from the point of view of the enthusiastic alumnus who roots for his college team, good or bad, out of loyalty and sentiment. Others are more like the professional gambler who cold-bloodedly examines the records of all the horses in the race and puts his money on the likely winners. These examples should be taken figuratively only, but in predicting future success, managers would do well to be more like the pro gambler than the loyal rooter.

Probably the first and most important thing for a manager to do is to recognize his limitations in predicting the future and do everything possible to gather accurate, relevant, representative information as a basis for his judgments. Let's look at the two problems separately—identification of potential for advancement and career counseling.

APPRAISAL OF POTENTIAL FOR ADVANCEMENT

This appraisal is essentially a four-part process, although the steps are not necessarily taken in the order that follows.

The manager first gathers information about the company's probable needs and their timing. These needs may be for specialized competence in technical fields as well as for new managerial talent. The probable timing affects the age range of those who might be considered and also places limitations on the action plans that might be developed to prepare candidates. As a second step the manager reviews the past performance of those who report to him—the things they have done well, the things for which they have not displayed much talent, and the things they could probably do weli if certain knowledge or experience deficiencies were overcome. A third step is to gather or update information regarding each person's career interests and his dedication to them. On the basis of all this information, as the fourth step, the manager makes a judgmental decision about the probability that a given employee will grow at a rate that will place him in competition for certain key openings in the future. Because of the relative inadequacy of this decision, it should be considered a short-term one, subject to frequent review as the future unfolds both for the firm and for the individual. Let's look at each of the four steps in the appraisal process in a little more detail.

WHAT WILL THE FIRM NEED?

Every individual has potential. Every individual has some area of talent that has not yet been fully developed. Every individual can probably add to his current knowledge and skill *in some way*. This is not the point. The point is whether his firm is likely to need growth along that line. This is the reason the manager needs to study—either by himself, with the help of staff, or with information from top management—the probable direction of business growth over the next five or ten years. Do the plans require growth, stability, or contraction in size? Do they anticipate product change, diversification, or continuance? Do they include more or less research and development, and in what fields? Are they based on changes in customers, in distribution methods? And, of course, what is the planned timetable? Factors such as these, translated into people terms and combined with data on turnover and retirement, provide the development goals against which the manager considers his employees.

For example, the XYZ Company, which has about 500 employees, makes and sells a product that is largely electromechanical. The research and development organization has recently evolved a chemical product to be used in conjunction with the normal product line. Market research indicates there are a number of additional profitable applications. Although some technical talent with the specific chemical background will need to be recruited for the technical staff, it is planned that the current sales and service organization will simply be asked to take on the new product line. The manager of this organization must therefore appraise the ability of current sales and

---

Steps in Appraising Potential for Advancement

1. Identify future company needs—both managerial and technical—and their probable timing.
2. Evaluate probable performance growth of current employees.
3. Consider known career goals of employees and extent of dedication to them.
4. Make judgmental decision regarding company career potential of each employee.

Since all factors change rapidly, review at least annually.

> ## Some Sources of Information About Future Company Needs
>
> 1. Planned growth of the business as a whole or some of its phases—or the lack of such planning.
> 2. Technology required for future products.
> 3. Functional emphasis of planned business changes —more research, engineering, manufacturing, marketing?
> 4. Probable external influencing factors, such as changes in customers, distributors, economic conditions, and competition.
> 5. Probable internal influencing factors, including changes in systems, work methods, cost control, acquisition and retention of employees, and productivity.
> 6. Changes in managing—increase or decrease in numbers of managers and changes in methods of managing.
> 7. Probable timing of each of these factors.
>
> Each of these should be reviewed at least annually.

service men to learn enough about the new product to be able to deal effectively with customers when it is ready for the market.

As another example, the ABC Division of a large manufacturing organization plans an expansion of facilities that includes establishment of a satellite plant in about two years. Both a plant manager and a staff of managers will be required to operate the new facility. So present managers are appraising the ability of current employees to develop managerial skills by the time the new plant will have opened its doors.

Again, because such plans often fail to materialize in exactly the way they are conceived or at the time originally predicted, these development goals need frequent review and revision. But the more specifically they are stated, the better the manager's appraisal of his employee's potential is likely to be. And conversely, the more vague and indefinite the goals are, the greater the appraisal error is likely to be.

ANALYZE PAST PERFORMANCE AND TRENDS

If a manager keeps a running account of how the employee is performing, or if at regular intervals he reviews the employee's progress against his work plan, this will be an especially valuable source of data. Of particular help in this step of the process is a focus on *trends* in the employee's performance. What has been improving rather well—or what has been deteriorating over time? Trends are important because they indicate the rate of the employee's growth in certain areas. And although it is never certain that he will continue at the same pace, the rate is unlikely to increase dramatically unless something is added to stimulate it—such as an incentive of some sort or the pressure of a heavier exposure to certain experiences. Basically, then, the manager is looking for clues to future performance by looking at past performance.

If a person has never had an opportunity to display his talents in a given area or there is no evidence available as to how successful he has been the manager makes a guess, looking at related activities. For example, if a person has been a technical contributor, working pretty much by himself without opportunity to display leadership qualities as such, the judgment as to whether he could learn to manage might be based on such evidence as the following: the relationship he has been able to establish with others who do related work or who use his work; the organizing abilities he displays in his own work; his ability to present, both orally and in writing, what he has been doing and the results he has achieved; his off-the-job participation in activities that offer leadership opportunity; and the extent to which he seeks such opportunities and is selected for them. None of these individually guarantees success as a manager, but if several are favorable, there is at least a reasonable basis for guessing that the potential is there. Small managing assignments then can test out the extent of that potential.

Unless the employee studied has reported to only one person, this analysis should not be the product of the current manager's thinking only. Instead he should actively seek the views, evaluations, and judgments of others who know the individual's work, his methods, his style, and other factors that might alter predictions. One manager's values almost certainly produce biased conclusions about an employee's potential.

For this reason, most organizations hold manpower reviews[1] periodically. At such reviews, managers at one level meet with their boss to discuss among themselves the relative qualifications of promising employees. This integration of several views by those who know the person provides better-balanced information, is fairer to the employee, and is more likely to be accurate in estimating future progress.

Another specialized and increasingly valued tool for illuminating potential for increased responsibility is the assessment center approach.[2] A group of employees, present or prospective, is studied intensively by a staff usually composed of professionals and line managers. Employee experience and interests are investigated through interview. Individual tests are administered to obtain data on planning and organization of work, intellectual level, and similar items. Group problem-solving exercises performed under observation yield information on behavioral patterns. When data generated during the session are combined with past performance ratings from previous managers, a very rich picture of capability and style is available to a manager or personnel department or both. It also provides to the individual a picture of himself relative to his peers that can be invaluable.

In any event, when by using every reasonable approach open to him a manager has put together an analysis of past performance on which to base estimates for the future, he is ready to meet with the employee to discuss his interests.

---

[1] See, for example, Walter R. Mahler and William F. Wrightnour, "Executive Continuity," Dow Jones–Irwin Inc., 1973.

[2] For detailed information, see Robert B. Finkle and William S. Jones, *Assessing Corporate Talent,* John Wiley & Sons, Inc., New York, 1970, and Douglas W. Bray, Richard J. Campbell, and Donald L. Grant, *Formative Years in Business,* John Wiley & Sons, Inc., New York, 1974.

KNOW EMPLOYEE'S CAREER INTERESTS

The manager's ability to get at the truth is severely limited by the nature of his relationship with the employee, the latter's receptivity to a discussion of the subject, and the extent to which he has evaluated his goals. If the relationship is poor, the help of a third party—a personnel development specialist or counselor—may be needed in order to get information. The problem of receptivity can be minimized if the manager makes a habit of discussing career regularly, perhaps annually while the man is in his 20s and 30s and at two-to-three-year intervals after that. If this has been done and the information has been documented, then even if a discussion comes when the man is reluctant to speak out, there is at least a reasonable chance that the manager will not be too badly misinformed.

The third barrier, however, is indeed serious. Many people simply do not know what they want to achieve in their working lives. The problem is not necessarily more severe when dealing with young men and women. Indeed, there is evidence of considerable mid-career unrest and indecision.[3] Seminars offered by professional consultants [4] to help participants set life goals can be helpful in such cases. It should be noted that a third-party catalyst, *not* the immediate manager, is practically a necessity. A manager helps himself as well as the employee by knowing about the availability of such workshops and referring employees to them when appropriate.

MAKE THE JUDGMENT

Having collected data now on (1) the future manpower needs of the business, (2) the performance strengths, weaknesses, and potential of reporting employees, and (3) their serious career interests, the manager can weigh his information

---

[3] George J. Berkwitt, "Management—Sitting on a Time Bomb?" *Dun's Review,* July 1972, pp. 38–41.
[4] For a description, see Richard C. Hodgson, "Who Are You? Where Are You Going?" *Business Quarterly,* Winter 1972, p. 11.

and make a judgmental decision as to which employees are likely candidates for future important positions in the company. In making this list of high-potential employees, it will be more useful if the manager indicates the kinds of positions for which he believes the employees have most potential. To document his judgment for future reference, the worksheet shown as Exhibit 5 may be utilized.

THE RUNNER-UP CHART

As a variation of the procedure just described, many companies have managers prepare runner-up charts for their organizations annually or biannually. The appraisal process is essentially the same except that instead of using future business needs as the developmental goal against which employees are appraised, the qualifications needed for the next higher job are detailed in a set of specifications (see Chapter 13), past performance and career interests are assessed, and the most likely two or three candidates are noted as possible successors. Frequently a color code is used to classify either the employee's readiness for the job or the time it would take to prepare him. (See Exhibit 6.)

APPRAISAL FOR CAREER COUNSELING

Career-counseling appraisal is the other side of the coin. Instead of describing company needs and then evaluating employees against these needs, the manager begins with the employee's demonstrated abilities and trends in performance. These form the basis on which the manager identifies future opportunities that might require the employee's unique combination of abilities and helps pinpoint some of the experiences that might lead toward these opportunities.

Because what they say may have such a profound effect on employees and because the area of career goals is so much a matter of individual prerogative, managers need to participate in such appraisals with humility and awareness of their own limitations. It is usually wise for a manager to place the responsibility both for the appraisal and for the subsequently devised plan of action in the hands of the employee. Under the circumstances, this kind of appraisal is not so much a guide for the manager's action as it is a help to the employee. It is therefore more likely to be successful and useful if the manager will consider his thoughts, suggestions, and view of the future as only one contribution to the employee's personal appraisal of his career possibilities. The starting point, following the employee's request to discuss the subject, is preparation on both sides.

The manager. The manager needs to review his notes on the performance of the employee, the things he has done well and not so well over the years, and any conditions—such as pressure or supervision—that seemed to make a difference in his performance. Especially important are changes or trends in performance or in ability to operate under more difficult conditions, which may indicate growth or lack of it. The manager needs to review both formal educational background and courses taken later on as a result of interest or felt work needs. He must consider whatever he can find out about the employee's off-the-job activities that might denote additional talents and interests, and he should formally consult his associate managers for their views of the employee and their estimates of his potential.

The next area of preparation is the classification of these abilities into possible future performance areas. For this step, the manager not only considers his own organization component and his own company but tries to think as well of other work toward which the employee might reasonably be expected to grow and for which there may be a future demand. He should take into account such factors as general economic changes, the possible emergence of new businesses, the effect of worldwide trade, and—within the company—possible changes in work methods, new products and marketing developments, and the company's projection of its manpower needs, both technical and managerial. From these factors he selects several that suggest promising career goals for the employee. Critical at this point is the manager's ability to anticipate future requirements and not suggest paths open today that may be closed by the time the employee is ready for them.

The third phase of the manager's preparation is to think through the additional knowledge and skill the employee may need to acquire, the experiences most likely to test him out and prepare him for promising opportunities. It is important for the manager to suspend judgment, for the time being, about the relative desirability of these growth alternatives so that he can describe them objectively without appearing to dictate the employee's future.

Finally, the manager needs to note the specific questions or points on which he wishes to obtain information from the employee. These should certainly include:

- ☐ The extent to which the employee's view of his performance and the conditions under which it is likely to be favorable agrees with the manager's own.
- ☐ The employee's career goals or interests and his seeming dedication to them.
- ☐ The degree of realism with which the employee appears to estimate his chances for future growth.
- ☐ The consistency of his career goals with the planned growth of the company.
- ☐ Opportunities that can be identified within the scope of the employee's current position for making a start toward career goals.
- ☐ Any help the employee expects or would like to receive from his manager with respect to his career efforts.

It is only fair to point out that while some managers are imaginative and broad-gauged in their thinking, many are far too limited. Some are so pressed for time that they are unable to give adequate consideration to a variety of employee career paths. It is of great importance that they convey this limitation to the employee, personally seek out other advice from associates or staff, and certainly suggest that the employee also do so for himself.

The employee. The employee needs to prepare, too. If he has opened the question of future opportunities with his manager, he needs to be ready to discuss his talents as he sees them and his career interests as he currently formulates them.

The first area for employee preparation is probably a review of his career to date, including how he feels about the various positions or assignments he has undertaken, what he has done well and what he has done badly, what he has enjoyed and has not enjoyed. Second, he should decide what kinds of work situations have contributed most—and least—to his productivity. For example, has he been most productive under the pressure of short-time schedules? Or when he could set a reasonable pace? Has his output increased when the work was highly structured and he could measure his results—or not? Has he done best under a strong, fairly dominant manager or under one who left him alone much of the time? This backward look should tell him something of his abilities and work performances.

Third, since no one is completely objective about himself, it is highly desirable that the employee who is serious about his career seek advice from a qualified third party about his areas of talent and strength. Vocational counseling agencies that combine a testing and counseling approach can often be most useful for this purpose. So can Veterans Administration offices, professional psychologists, and the psychology departments of colleges and universities, which frequently offer their services not only to their own students but to adults in the community as well. In all probability the name of a competent agency or individual can be obtained from the company's personnel department. Findings and recommendations from such a source should not be given excessive weight but should simply be considered as one more input to the employee's thinking about himself and his probable future.

The fourth area of preparation for the employee is the

consideration of trends in the world today that could affect his career choice and the identification of various positions or fields of work in which he feels he could and would like to fit. The fifth area is the identification of what he would need to know, and know how to do, in order to fill these jobs successfully and the evaluation in at least a preliminary fashion of whether the additional knowledge and skills would be worth the sacrifice of time and effort on his part.

As a final step, the employee needs to formulate the specific points on which he wishes to secure the manager's opinion or commitment of positive help. He will probably have these questions:

- ☐ How closely does the manager's opinion of his performance and desirable work situation agree with his own?
- ☐ What business-oriented translation or interpretation can the manager make of the vocational counselor's findings, if such an expert has been consulted?
- ☐ What is the manager's estimate of the employee's relative ability to achieve his tentative career goals, and what other possibilities does the manager feel he might consider?
- ☐ What additional light can the manager shed on the requirements of possible positions and ways of meeting these requirements?
- ☐ What opportunities are there within his current responsibilities and within his current organization for making a start toward meeting these requirements?

When the work of preparation has been completed (Exhibit 7 may serve as a guide), manager and employee are ready to exchange information, opinions, and speculations with a view to helping the employee appraise himself as a first step in planning his own career.

Appraisal of employee potential is an attempt to estimate future position requirements and probable employee growth and to match the two. It can be made productive for the organization if information regarding business plans is translated carefully into people terms and if individual past performance, performance trends, demonstrated talents, and career interests are then considered in this framework. It can be made useful to the employee by helping him review his demonstrated abilities, rate of growth, and career interests and by contributing to his identification of possible career directions through a joint assessment of the requirements of these alternatives and of the availability of experience, training, and other preparation for meeting these requirements.

chapter 12

After appraising potential, what?

IF IT IS WORTH THE EFFORT TO APPRAISE EMPLOYEES' potential, it should be worth doing something about it.

After a manager has listed his most promising employees and has prepared his runner-up charts and passed them along to his boss or the personnel department, he has a number of decisions to make. Should he tell the men they are listed? What record should he keep, not only about these individuals but also about those who failed to make the list? What about the others—what effects will leakage of information about the list have on their attitudes, performance, and interest in the firm? And finally, what positive action will be constructive both for those who are listed and for those who are not?

SHOULD AN EMPLOYEE KNOW HE IS ON THE
HIGH-POTENTIAL LIST?

There are both advantages and disadvantages in telling an employee he is on the high-potential list. The advantages are that an employee is usually pleased at the news, may respond with even greater dedication to his work, and views his place on the list as recognition and reward for past efforts. The disadvantages are that he sometimes begins to expect rapid promotion and, if it does not occur soon, may become disgruntled, feel short-changed, and leave for another department or company that he feels offers him the advancement he has come to feel is his right. Occasionally an individual may react by losing interest in his present assignment so that his performance deteriorates; or he may feel he has it made, with the same unfortunate result. When other employees learn by inference that they were not selected, they may become discouraged and feel they have no future. Or the so-called promotables may tell others of their favored position, with negative effects on their associates.

Probably the most usual practice is for managers *not* to discuss their promotable list with employees who are on it on the grounds that the disadvantages outweigh the advantages. There are problems with this practice, however. Once the manager has made his choices, his decision usually shows in his attitude and behavior. For example, he may broaden the responsibilities of certain employees. Or the level of his communication with them may move up. In various ways, other employees may begin to sense a sort of "in" group. Then, too, almost inevitably employees learn somehow that managers have been asked to submit promotable lists or runner-up charts periodically; and as they begin to speculate about the names included, some insecure feelings may result. Excellent employees, fearing they have not been given favorable consideration, may actively seek other employment.

Some compromise, therefore, is probably desirable. A reasonable one is for the manager to tell all his promotable employees, not just those listed for upper management's attention, that he feels they have a good future. One way of doing this, if he holds regular reviews of each employee's work, is to lean back in his chair at the close of the session and say something like this: "Joe, I'm very pleased with your work. When we talk about individual performance, we usually look at aspects of it that are in trouble or need special attention, and so it's easy to get the impression that we only notice what's wrong. I want to be sure that you know we see the good things, too. I'm very pleased with what you're doing, and I've brought your accomplishments to the attention of my boss. He feels as I do that you're making an excellent contribution and should have a very good future with us. Naturally no one can say just how that future will unfold, but continuing to do excellent work on this job is certainly the best way to be sure you'll be considered for advancement when the right opportunity comes along."

In this way, the employee knows that his work is appreciated and is considered valuable and that two levels of management recognize his ability. Without making any commitment about a next job, the manager keeps the employee focused on the need for excellence in his current assignments.

For other employees—those whose future appears more limited or who are not yet on top of their present jobs—the manager continues to focus on performance improvement as discussed in earlier chapters.

SHOULD THE MANAGER KEEP RECORDS?

To make his appraisal decisions about employees' potential, the manager will have collected information on past performance and trends in performance, talents not yet demonstrated, capability as a manager and as an individual worker, and career interests and plans. These data should certainly be retained, together with the evidence on which the conclusions or judgments were based. Not only will they be useful the next time a similar appraisal is made, but they are also invaluable in helping formulate plans to improve the employee's performance or add to his responsibilities in some way. Whether the manager keeps the records himself or sends them along to the personnel department depends on company practice. But in either case they should be readily accessible to the manager so that he will indeed refer to them and use them.

A good rule of thumb for personnel records, wherever they are kept, is to retain factual or objective data as long as the individual is employed but to retain documented judgmental conclusions only on a current basis.

WHAT ABOUT THOSE NOT LISTED AS PROMOTABLE?

A manager can ease the probable unfavorable effect on those not considered most promotable by setting up the whole system properly in the first place. He should, as a start, let his employees know that he regularly selects individuals who may become candidates for higher positions. This seems desirable not only because the activity involved in collecting information, completing charts or forms, and so on is likely to be noticed but especially because, in the right setting, the manager can turn this practice into an effective tool for improved relations with employees. The procedure should preferably be mentioned several months before appraisals or runner-up charts are due so that it is obvious the manager is under no pressure to explain his actions and so that employees have time to absorb the idea, discuss it, and ask questions about it. The employees should be told (1) the reason for the practice, (2) management's intent with respect to it, (3) advantages to the individual, (4) advantages to the company, (5) how the list will be used, (6) who has access to it, and (7) how employees can get the most from it. Thus:

1. *Reason for the practice.* The firm is interested in making sure that a very important resource, its employees, will be ready with the qualifications needed at the time business plans require them.

2. *Management intent.* The list is intended as a safeguard to insure that capable individuals are not overlooked or excluded from consideration as openings occur because they are in a different part of the business or because they have not

been identified soon enough to receive the necessary experience. The list is reviewed periodically, and the names on it may well be changed as employees respond to new hurdles and challenges and as business needs become more specific. It is not intended as a fixed, exclusive list that prohibits others from competing for openings. On the contrary, opportunity for advancement is still available to all employees, and qualification for a given opening will be the most important criterion for selection.

3. *Advantages to the individual.* The practice demonstrates the company's desire to give employees first consideration for better jobs. It assures the individual that his career, not just his current assignment, is of interest to management. It helps insure that employees in large organizations are not lost because they are in small plants or slow-growing parts of the company.

4. *Advantages to the company.* It keeps managers alert to the progress of promising employees, makes them aware of strengths and deficiencies, helps them make their business plans on a sounder basis. It provides direction for recruiting, training, and other developmental programs.

5. *How the list will be used.* The list will be referred to when promotions and transfers are to be made but will not determine who will be selected for a given position. Such decisions will be made only at the time of the opening in the light of the position requirements as they exist and of the qualifications of all eligible employees at that time, regardless of whether or not they are on the list.

6. *Who has access to it.* Except for the managers who prepare and submit the information and those who receive and study it, only those who are charged with its safekeeping or analysis will have access to the list.

7. *How employees can get the most from it.* An employee can help his manager make sounder decisions in a number of ways. The first is to give excellent performance and sustain it. He can also document his work accomplishments

periodically and submit the information to his manager in writing;[1] he can make certain this his manager is aware of any self-development activities he undertakes; he can discuss his career goals with his manager from time to time; and, specifically, he can inquire about other positions for which he feels qualified. If he is a professional worker, he can enhance his professional reputation by publishing articles and delivering papers before his colleagues. He can cooperate with his manager in undertaking such additional responsibilities in his current job as his manager feels is wise—responsibilities that may add to his qualifications for other work.

In summary. Probably the most important single point to be made is that the promotable or runner-up list is not a "go, no-go" list, that those not on it are not excluded from advancement and those on it are not assured advancement. It is merely the manager's best thoughtful guess about the current state of employee qualifications. The guess will without question change as the situation develops.

If the aspects of listing high-potential individuals described here are discussed thoroughly and put into administrative practice, the response of most employees will be favorable.

WHAT CONSTRUCTIVE ACTION CAN THE MANAGER TAKE?

By far the most important action for the manager is to note any significant suspected or demonstrated employee strengths not now being used. He should also note areas of knowledge, skill, or experience that could be improved within the general scope of the employee's current assignment. *Whether or not the employee is listed as high-potential,* if his performance is within satisfactory limits these two areas provide points of focus for the manager's coaching efforts and can be tackled as outlined in Chapter 5. The result should be a second set of action plans structured on a career look at the

---

[1] For instructions on preparing such a list, see Marion S. Kellogg, *When Man and Manager Talk,* Gulf Publishing Co., Houston, 1969, p. 97.

employee. These will supplement the earlier plans that were made on the basis of his present job.

If the firm is serious about getting its manpower resources ready to meet business challenges, there should also be a series of planned activities, both group and individual, including special training and job movement for those on the high-potential list who are likely to benefit. Some of these steps may take selected employees outside the current manager's organization, or he may be asked to help in training and developing employees not now in his group. These activities will probably be initiated by top management or by the personnel department.

Now that special emphasis is being placed on accelerating the professional and management careers of minority employees and women, managers have special responsibilities for taking constructive actions with these employees. Assuming potential for advancement exists, the key probably lies in deliberate, periodic job change in order to widen and deepen knowledge, skill, and experience. But to accomplish what is needed will take forthright, explicit feedback on a continuing, day-to-day basis. In this way, as the employee is thrust more rapidly than normal into new work responsibilities, he receives very clear, rapid information on what he is doing right and what needs to be changed if he is to be successful. For managers to do this, they must have dedication, sincere interest, and a *way* of providing the feedback that displays their support, confidence, and desire to help.

CAREER COUNSELING

It is important that each manager make and implement plans to fulfill his responsibility to contribute to the development of *all* his employees. In many cases, the springboard for his activity in this regard will be some form of career counseling.

The impetus for career counseling may come either from the person who wants to know what his opportunities for advancement are or from the manager who recognizes that the employee must cooperate by taking certain steps toward his own development. Essential to a meaningful career-counseling session is a sound relationship of mutual respect. If either party feels the other is not to be trusted or is incompetent, it is unlikely that much constructive action will result.

The essential difference between a work-coaching and career-counseling session is that in the first the manager has primary responsibility for the decisions and for the quality of work that results since he is responsible for the performance of his organization. In the career-counseling session, however, the primary responsibility for the decisions is the employee's. The manager is available to give opinions, advice, and information from his own perspective. But whether the employee chooses to accept and use them is part of his responsibility to himself. His career, his future are his to manage. For this reason, the counseling session needs to be structured so that the manager's comments supplement—but do not dominate or supplant—the employee's appraisal of his abilities and his career potential and so that they contribute to the employee's plans with respect to his growth and possible career. The manager needs to make this point clear so that the employee will expect to play a leading role in the session.

Prior to their meeting, each party should prepare for the discussion in roughly the fashion outlined in the preceding chapter. Here is a likely format:

1. *The manager sets the stage.* The manager reaffirms that this discussion is primarily to help the employee appraise or reappraise his career situation and arrive at sound plans for action. He makes it clear that everyone has different objectives for himself. For some, career growth may mean continuing to improve in their present jobs; for others it may mean upward movement in the organization; for still others it may mean quite dramatic changes in field. Each person needs to decide what he feels is right for him. The manager hopes he can add some things that the employee will find useful in making his decisions and that from the discussion the employee will find ways in which

the manager can be of positive help within the framework of the present job.

2. *The employee assesses his career to date.* The manager suggests that the employee begin by reviewing his career to date: what work he has done well and liked most, in what atmosphere he has worked best, and so on. The manager listens attentively and asks questions from time to time to bring out performance strengths and weaknesses, work likes and dislikes, and when possible, reasons for them.

3. *The manager supplements the career assessment.* When the employee completes his analysis, or as opportunity arises, the manager adds any important factors the employee may have overlooked, especially if they represent talents on which to build. A good way to do this is to make the point, say why it seems to be true, and ask the employee to consider it to see if he agrees.

4. *They discuss third-party recommendations.* The manager asks if the employee has talked with a vocational counselor or personnel development specialist or whether he has had career recommendations from other managers. If so, and if he would like to talk about them, the manager would be glad to add these thoughts to the picture. If the manager has consulted former supervisors or associates or other professionals, he may also wish to introduce their thoughts and comments at this point.

5. *The manager summarizes the employee's talents for career building.* The manager then works with the employee to summarize what appear to be the major talents on which to build his career. If there are important deficiencies that are difficult or impossible to overcome and that would rule out certain career areas, these too are noted. In general, however, it is wiser to encourage the employee to focus on existing talents, knowledge, and experience and make plans to add to these resources. For example, if the employee has been educated in business administration and has had sound experience in general and

cost accounting, these are most probably the assets on which to build. He may choose to broaden into tax accounting or apply his accounting know-how to a different kind of business or product. He may consider supervising some accounting work if there is reason to believe he has managerial potential. But a sudden desire to manage a technical project requiring extensive engineering knowledge is probably unrealistic unless he is willing to undertake the long effort of acquiring an engineering education at that point and unless there is reason to believe that he possesses strong aptitudes for mathematics and engineering as well as the potential for managing.

6. *The employee expresses his career interests.* The manager then draws out the employee, encouraging him to express his career interests and the kinds of positions he would seriously like to hold and for which he believes he could qualify in the next few years. He should think about field of work, about level in the organization, and about kind of business or product association.

7. *The manager describes business needs.* To the extent he is able to do so, the manager describes what he believes will be the future needs of the firm and of his organization as they pertain to the employee's talents and expressed career interests. He makes it clear that this is an area of speculation and opinion only. To whatever extent he can, he may also describe anticipated events in the economy, in the country, and in technology generally that could affect the employee's career choices. He offers these for the employee's consideration only. He cannot make guarantees for the future.

8. *The manager summarizes career alternatives and implications.* The manager then works with the employee to list what appear to be his most promising career alternatives. Together they identify the knowledge, skill, and experience the employee should add to his current know-how in order to compete for appropriate positions.

9. *They discuss additional questions.* Either may want to raise questions for discussion and comment. At such a time

the manager should do his best to supply useful information but should avoid taking on the employee's rightful responsibility for reaching his own decisions and solving his own problems.

10. *They agree on action plans.* If the session has been such that agreement is possible on specific actions each party should undertake, these should be noted. The employee's action plan will be part of his self-development design. The manager's action plan will contribute to the employee's development and will focus on actions he can take within the framework of the employee's present job and their present relationship. For example, he might agree to enlarge responsibilities in certain ways, to provide added coaching in certain areas, to explore other positions with his own boss or his associates. These are within his control. He should not, however, agree to move the employee to a new position in two years, since he cannot commit himself to something outside his control.

It should be recognized that such counseling may take more than one meeting. Time for thoughtful reflection may be desirable for both parties. This is not a subject for hasty conclusions.

Outline for Career-Counseling Discussion

1. The manager sets the stage.
2. The employee assesses his career to date.
3. The manager supplements the career assessment.
4. They discuss third-party recommendations.
5. The manager summarizes the employee's talents for career building.
6. The employee expresses his career interests.
7. The manager describes business needs.
8. The manager summarizes career alternatives and implications.
9. They discuss additional questions.
10. They agree on action plans.

It should also be recognized that sometimes a manager or supervisor is not able to carry out such a discussion. He may not feel he knows the employee well enough, the relationship between them may not be good enough, or his awareness of career possibilities for the employee may not be sound enough. When this is the case, it is better to avoid the discussion and refer the employee to a qualified member of the personnel staff or an outside vocational counselor. One of the responsibilities of higher-level management is to be aware of the ability of managers or supervisors who contribute to employee development. Where there is a deficiency, other means should be devised for getting this important work done—help from a personnel specialist or consultant or some other special assistance should be supplied to make up for this missing managerial skill.

Here are a few do's and don'ts for managers to keep in mind during a discussion:

Do	Don't
Prepare thoughtfully for the meeting.	Give spur-of-the-moment, offhand, or casual opinions and advice.
Provide facts, information, suggestions, opinions, help based on personal experience.	Make decisions for the employee or attempt to solve his problems.
Contribute to the employee's appraisal and action plans.	Make the appraisal and action plan for the employee.
Give honest estimates of observed performance strengths and deficiencies.	Overstate the employee's abilities in an effort to be kind and encouraging.
Emphasize the importance of building a career around the employee's talents and strengths.	Emphasize deficiencies that may be difficult or impossible to overcome.
Make commitments about changes in position responsibilities or other developmental actions only if they are within control.	Discuss the future in such a way that the employee is led to expect certain actions that may be beyond the individual manager's control.

Do	Don't
Explore alternate paths of advancement.	Focus on a single, narrow career goal that may turn out to be unacceptable, unachievable, or unavailable.
Make it clear when what is being said is not fact but opinion or estimate or forecast.	Give the impression of knowing what is best for the employee. No manager knows what future events will be.
Base suggestions on what things are expected to be like in the future.	Let personal experiences or current business needs (which may be changing) unduly influence recommendations.
Ask questions to draw out employee's appraisal of himself and his career goals and plans.	Talk too much.

During the session, the manager should make notes for later reference on—

- ☐ The extent to which the employee's analysis of his performance strengths and deficiencies agrees with his own.
- ☐ The insight the employee displays with respect to his talents and probable potential.
- ☐ The employee's expressed career goals and any decisions made with respect to them.
- ☐ The extent to which the employee's career goals are consistent with the plans of the firm and his organization.
- ☐ Additional knowledge, skill, and experience needed to move toward career goals.
- ☐ Opportunities available within the scope of the employee's current position for making a start toward his career goals.
- ☐ Specific developmental actions agreed to.
- ☐ Checkpoint dates when some review of developmental actions or of career situation will be desirable.

Specifically this information provides additional data to be factored into later appraisals of the employee's potential and, more importantly, into the manager's coaching practices with respect to the employee. To the extent the employee is performing his current job well, the manager may now begin to add responsibilities that will take him in the direction of his career goals.

Managers should let all employees whose work is excellent know their efforts are appreciated and a good future is anticipated for them. At the same time, it should be made clear that listing as promotable or as a runner-up for a higher position neither guarantees promotion nor excludes those not listed from consideration when openings occur. Managers should use data from appraisal of potential as another input for their coaching activity and as a basis for counseling employees about various possible career paths and requirements for advancement.

chapter 13

Appraising candidates for promotion

ONE OF THE MOST LONGED-FOR AND YET DREADED EVENTS IN A manager's life is the need to fill an open position reporting to him. It is at one time or another longed for because no employee, regardless of his competence, completely satisfies a manager's expectations. A new person might improve on the old ways of doing things or take advantage of opportunities that have been allowed to slip by. But an open position is dreaded too, because the search for competence is difficult, and the break-in time seems endlessly annoying and burdensome.

Every manager knows an open position represents an opportunity to improve his organization's output. Too often he fills it as quickly as possible only to discover afterward that, far from adding to output, the new employee has faced him with a set of problems that demand his attention and subtract from his overall managing time.

A relatively small amount of effort spent in advance of selecting the new person would greatly reduce this disappointment and, as a minimum, place the manager in the position of knowing just about how much help, and what kind, the employee will need for an efficient transition.

APPRAISING THE JOB REQUIREMENTS

The manager will probably consider several candidates, all of whom possess some qualifications for the job but probably none of whom has all of them. Also, some of the candidates will probably come from within the manager's own organization, some from other departments in the company, and some from outside. Presumably, the personnel department has done some preliminary screening, and the manager's choice has been narrowed to three or four candidates. The problem now is to make a relative appraisal of their qualifications and choose the one most likely to fill the position successfully.

The manager starts with the open position itself. What are the current and future problems of the position, and what is to be accomplished in the next year or two? What knowledge must the person have if he is to achieve these goals? What skills? What interests or attitudes are needed? What previous work experience would be useful?

As an example, suppose a product engineer is needed for a line of small household appliances. The line lacks a fresh look, although the functioning level is good and complaints and service requests are low. Costs must come down, though, if the products are to remain competitive. Some improvement in appearance, in ease of handling, and in cost could probably be achieved through substitutions in materials—the introduction of plastics, for example. Such changes would have to be followed through the shop rather carefully during the initial stages, and since some alteration of factory equipment and tooling

---

Checklist to Establish Job Requirements

Work Requirements

1. Specific short-range results.
2. Specific long-range results.
3. Specific problems.

Personal Requirements

1. Technical knowledge and skill.
2. Product knowledge.
3. Knowledge of company.
4. Customer knowledge.
5. Knowledge of tools, work methods, equipment.
6. Managerial or supervisory skill.
7. Financial knowledge and skill.
8. Skill in contacting others.

---

would be necessary, the product engineer would be expected to put together the total cost picture in order to sell management on the desirability of investing the necessary capital.

These requirements mean that the person who fills this position should have a good background in electromechanical engineering; sufficient knowledge of materials (especially the newer plastics) to be able to identify those that are suitable for the product; demonstrated talent for design (including appearance) of small gadgets; basic understanding of costs and demonstrated ability to estimate costs accurately; demonstrated contact skills with both factory personnel and upper echelons of management; and reasonable persuasiveness and fluency in a situation in which he has had time to prepare himself.

APPRAISING THE SITUATIONAL FACTORS

Next, the manager considers the situation in which the employee will probably find himself, the environment in which he'll be working. What time pressures are there? What limitations on money, people, other resources? What sort of priority will his responsibilities have? What is the status of the work? Is it going well, so that his job will be to sustain progress? Or is it going badly, so that he must turn the situation around? In what phase is it: just starting, midway, or nearing the end? What sorts of associates will he have: experienced workers who will be able to help him, or people who are also new in their jobs and may be quite competitive in their attitude toward him? What is the manager like: what sort of standards and ways of managing does he have? Will the new subordinate have people working for him directly? Will he have access to help from technicians or secretarial pools?

Factors such as these place pressures of one sort or another on the person who takes the position. They need to be translated, in a general way, into a description of conditions that he should have a demonstrated ability to handle—or at least he should not have shown repeated inability to handle them earlier in his career. Managers are prone to overlook such situational factors, perhaps because they are so used to living with them that they lose their awareness of them. And yet these

---

Checklist to Establish Situational Requirements

Time available to produce results.
Availability of resources: manpower, money, tools, and
    equipment.
Priority of work.
Current status of work:
    Beginning, midway, or ending.
    Satisfactory or unsatisfactory.
    Improving or deteriorating.
    Expanding or contracting.
Limitations on authority.
Competitive situation.   ⎤
Customer situation.   ⎬ Inside or outside
Supplier or vendor situation. ⎦   the company
Managing style of boss.
Characteristics and qualifications of associates.
Qualifications of reporting employees.

factors change the character of a job quite radically and often prove to be a source of selection mistakes.

A man who putters away in his own basement perfecting a gadget may produce an excellent product. The same man, told to produce a new gadget within one month, work with the factory to get it made properly, and feed his cost data to a computer for analysis, may be totally unable to function. Yet in each case the output is the same. It is the situational factors, the conditions under which the output is produced, that differ.

A field salesman for one line of a company's products, used to managing his own time with considerable freedom and required to do little paperwork other than supplying proof of orders, may find himself in trouble if asked to supply a detailed weekly sales plan each Monday morning and a Friday write-up of each contact made during the week—besides serving as the telephone coordination point for all inquiries in his territory about *all* the company's products. The latter job requires much more planning and clerical skill, broader product knowledge, and specific organizing skills entirely missing from the former job. Yet the expected accomplishments may sound almost alike.

Let's go back to the earlier example of the product engineer, make some guesses about the situational factors on his job, and see what qualifications they add to the list. Let's suppose a competitor has unexpectedly introduced a new, very attractive, directly competitive product line so that time is of great importance if the company is not to lose its sales position. Let's say, too, that the factory is in the midst of a tooling changeover for another product line and will not look with any enthusiasm on a second major change. Let's say the product engineer will have no employees working for him but will be expected to get personnel assigned from other parts of the organization as needed.

Just these three situational factors stiffen the requirements. The management under the circumstances cannot afford much risk with the new employee. Since time is so important, he should already have displayed or demonstrated excellent gadgeteering and appearance-design abilities. The factory situation implies that he will have to be both convincing in getting personnel to do what he wants and aggressive in getting reasonable priority assigned to his work. And the employee situation also implies a certain experience in getting what he needs, a personal sense of urgency that he is able to communicate to others, and an ability to obtain his own boss's help when he is unable to get something accomplished for himself. But he must be able to do this without being considered a cry baby or a squealer or being described in any number of other unattractive terms. Given these conditions, the needs of the open position emerge more clearly:

KNOWLEDGE
Electromechanical engineering.
Materials, especially qualities of plastics.
Simple cost accounting and cost estimation.

SKILL
Gadget design previously demonstrated.
Appearance design previously demonstrated.
Factory contact.
Upper management contact.
Product presentation.

PERSONAL QUALITIES
Ability to influence factory management to do what is necessary when it is necessary.
Ability to get other managers to assign high priorities to his work.
Ability to get needed decisions from higher management without antagonizing associates.
Ability to impart own sense of urgency to others.

This list of specifications is probably incomplete. Imaginary cases necessarily are. In actual situations, too, it is almost impossible to itemize *every* requirement. But if the manager will carefully review the job and the conditions under which it is to be accomplished and be sure he has listed the most important, highest-priority items, he will have contributed a great deal to the ultimate selection of the man who is best qualified to do the job.

APPRAISING CANDIDATE QUALIFICATIONS

Having appraised the work and the situation, the manager now turns his attention to the candidates in an effort to make a relative appraisal of the extent to which each meets the specifications.

This appraisal consists of a careful, step-by-step review of what can be learned about candidates with respect to each item in the specification. It is slow, thorough detective work. When the earlier analysis was made of the work and the situation surrounding it, it was the manager who made the most important contribution to it. He could be helped only a little by a personnel or administrative specialist who could take a more objective look at the manager himself or at some of the charac-

---

Sources of Data About Candidates

Application blanks or résumés.
Company personnel files.
Company payroll files.
Company training records.
Employee appraisal records.
Comments of former employers.
Comments of former associates.
Samples of past work.
Formal test data. (See footnote.)
Personal interview data.
Community, professional, and other off-the-job activities.
Credit checks.
Educational records.
College yearbook showing campus activities.
Comments of teachers and professors.

Note: The value of school and college data probably decreases with time.

teristics of the men reporting to him. Much of the fact finding about the candidates in this phase of the appraisal, however, *can* be done by a third person and submitted for the manager's review and decision.

Since not every organization supplies this help, it is perhaps worth reviewing how information can reasonably be obtained and how it can be made as accurate as possible. The manager needs (1) factual data relating to education and work history, such as might be found in standard personnel files or in résumés; (2) evaluation of past performance—that is, exhibited skills and personal qualities—obtainable from documented employee appraisal forms, discussion with former employers, and actual exhibits or samples of the candidates' work; (3) estimates of potential not yet demonstrated, obtained by inference from off-the-job activities, expressed interests, and tests of aptitude; [1] and finally (4) face-to-face impressions, exhibited personal qualities and abilities, self-reported accomplishments, and career interests, as obtained in personal interviews.

Education and work history. As a first step in evaluating the qualifications of each candidate, the manager looks at the paper record against already established specifications. Have the candidate's education and work experience exposed him to the necessary technical information and the work problems he would face in the open position? Has his education been recent, or has work in the years since his education been such as to keep him abreast of *current* knowledge and techniques? Has the candidate refreshed and updated his knowledge by taking extra courses, participating in professional organizations, and similar activities? Exposure to required knowledge and opportunity to demonstrate skill are not guarantees that candidates actually possess the knowledge and skill, but they are a necessary beginning. Often paperwork—personnel records or résumés—will

---

[1] It should be noted that recent legislation requires that tests be validated as job-related if they are used to eliminate candidates from consideration for positions. See, for example, Donald J. Petersen, "The Impact of Duke Power on Testing," *Personnel,* March–April 1974, p. 30.

not give sufficient information to evaluate this point. A helpful addition is to request of each candidate a brief history of the work accomplishments he considers most significant throughout his career. He should be asked to describe the problems he faced in enough detail to show their difficulty, then describe what *he* did to solve them and what results he achieved or what their impact was on the organization. These will need to be verified later but will help in eliciting information about some of the situations in which the employee has worked, as well as determining his exposure to relevant work experience.

Evaluation of past performance. Having determined to some extent the candidate's previous exposure to needed knowledge and experience as well as something of the conditions under which he has performed, the manager now needs an evaluation of how well he has applied his knowledge, what skill he displayed, and how he responded to the conditions in which he was working. If the candidate now works for the manager or has done so in the past, much of this information is already known. If the man is employed elsewhere in the company, a first step is to examine whatever data are in the personnel files, appraisal forms, and other records. It must be remembered, though, that these may give a reasonable picture of the man, but they usually do so from the frame of reference of the former manager and in the context of the old position. Since the manager needs to keep his eyes firmly fixed on the work of the *new* position, he should supplement the written information with personal discussions with former employers. If the candidate is employed elsewhere, a check will need to be made with former employers to whatever extent the candidate will permit.

The ability to get needed information in such a discussion is a skill in itself. The following approach is recommended, preferably in person or, if necessary, by phone: (1) As an introduction, explain that the former employee is being considered for an open position. Leave the position unspecified initially. (2) Ask for an accurate description of what the person was assigned to do and how he did it. (3) Request answers to a few specific questions as to his skills and personal qualities. (4) Ask for an overall estimate of his ability to do the work of the open position (now described).

The objective throughout the discussion, and particularly in the second part, is to *get the facts* about what the person did under his previous manager, how he did it, under what conditions, and with what results. This information can then be translated thus: "Will I require him to do the same or similar things? Are his methods compatible with what I need? How effectively did he function under the former work conditions, and are the conditions in my organization the same or similar?" This information is generally far more useful than asking "Is the person any good? Could he do this new job?" Such general questions usually produce a mishmash of responses expressing the former manager's value judgments, which may be incompatible with the values and standards of the manager who has the opening. The recommended "just tell me what he did" approach may also help eliminate personal bias.

If the description of what the individual has done in the past does not include all the items listed as important in the specification, the manager then asks specifically about the remaining items. "What about his gadgeteering ability; have you seen anything of this? What about his skill in contacting factory personnel? Has he had to do any of that, or not? And with what success?" In each case, the manager tries to pin down just what the person did that displayed the skill or quality in question. This gives him the opportunity to evaluate its similarity or applicability to his own opening.

Finally, the manager describes the open position briefly and asks for an estimate of the candidate's ability to do it well. This usually produces rather general comments but may also bring out valid intuitive judgments, based on close association, that would be useful primarily as points to be verified through other means.

Throughout this discussion the man's history of accomplishment may serve as a basis for questioning should the former manager find it difficult to remember specific assignments. The manager may also be able to verify the magnitude of an employee's reported accomplishments that could be significant for the open job.

It is probably wise to check with all previous managers, but more recent ones should be more thoroughly interviewed. In the case of a candidate from outside the company, often the current employer cannot be contacted because the candidate does not want it known that he is looking for another job. Because this eliminates a most important source of information, the manager must explore the current position in greater depth than usual during his personal interview with the candidate.

Estimate of potential. It seldom happens that all the specifications for the open position have been met in former jobs. Usually there are certain skills that have not yet been exhibited, certain personal qualities about which former managers are in disagreement, certain situations the employee has not yet had to face. The manager needs to guess about these, and it is helpful to have some basis for his guesses. The personnel record or résumé or accomplishment history may give some clues from listed off-the-job activities and interests. For example, if the position requires great detail-mindedness and there is no evidence in the work record of this but the person has been secretary or treasurer of civic or professional associations, there is at least a clue that he possesses this quality.

In the case of the product design engineer, if a candidate has never had a work opportunity to make a business presentation persuasively and his off-the-job activity has consisted largely of puttering around in his basement making model airplanes, the chances are that he will need coaching in this area. If, on the other hand, he has helped Junior Achievement groups to put together their budget presentations, it is a little more likely that he will be able to master this aspect of his job fairly quickly. These are guesses, though, and subject to considerable error. They need verification through discussions with others who know the man, through personal interview with the man himself, and, for certain kinds of potential, perhaps through formal job-related testing.

Formal testing of the standardized variety is the province of the psychologist or trained personnel specialist. The manager could consult such a specialist, if one is available in the company, or make use of a reputable consulting psychologist for help in estimating potential in specific areas. There are two workable approaches. He may present his main specifications for the open position and ask which factors the specialist is able to help him measure or evaluate. Alternatively, he may discuss with the psychologist what he has already learned from personnel records and former managers and ask whether the specialist can help resolve some of the points that are uncertain or controversial. In either case, if the specialist believes tests can supply useful, indicative information, the candidate takes the tests under the direction of a trained test administrator who provides standard conditions and who then relays and interprets the test results, with some indication of probable accuracy.[2] To the manager, these test data represent more evidence to be added to his collection of information. Like other pieces of information, they will probably confirm some findings and raise questions about others. Confirmation is of course helpful, but questions are also frequently useful, since, in attempting to resolve them, the manager often uncovers situational factors that had escaped his attention before.

For example, if formal tests indicate a person is poor in dealing with numbers but previous supervisors have noted that his budget and cost work have been excellent, this discrepancy should be investigated with the former employers or with the candidate himself. It may turn out that he has done very little numerical work in past positions but has made skillful use of the accounting department or of clerical personnel. When this proves to be the case, the manager is in a position to decide if

---

[2] Because of the cultural bias implicit in some tests, legislation requires that tests used should be proven, valid predictors of job success or failure.

this sort of supporting help will be available in the open job. If it is, there is no problem. If it is not, he must decide whether this item is of sufficient importance to exclude the person from further consideration or whether other factors are so favorable that he is personally willing to contribute more to this aspect of the work.

The ability to estimate an individual's potential to do new things or to work under new conditions is without question the weakest link in a manager's ability to make sound selection decisions. For this reason every scrap of information contributing to this area becomes important. And information relating to off-the-job activities, formal test results, and questions raised by test data can be amplified and made more useful through fuller exploration during the personal interview.

Personal interview. This is frequently the greatest time waster in the manager's search for qualified candidates. The most obvious reason is that the manager is often diverted by something about the candidate and fails to pursue his careful evaluation. The distraction may be the candidate's appearance, some common interest they share, some likeness to a former employee, or any of a variety of biases or prejudices of which the manager may not even be consciously aware. The result is that the halo effect takes over, and everything about the candidate is rated higher or lower than it should be, depending on the direction of the manager's bias.

The second greatest time waster is that the manager so dominates the interview, talks so much, is so directive in his questions that the candidate has no opportunity to reveal his personal qualities or even to enlarge upon his previous experiences.

Both these hazards can be minimized if the manager will remind himself that his is a detective role in this situation and prepare himself rather carefully. He should review the personal specifications and reflect on the information already gathered about the candidate on each item. He should make notes of items about which there is little or no information as well as those for which information to date has been contradictory or controversial. He should then plan his interview so as to have the candidate display, as far as possible, these qualities or skills. Usually the best way to find out if certain qualifications are met is to ask the candidate to display his skill or give a demonstration or a sample.

To use the product engineer as an example once more, the manager could describe a typical materials problem and ask the candidate what plastic he would recommend. This would reveal whether the man knows his way around the standard handbooks and what information about the specs of various plastics is at his fingertips. A sample of his work would show whether his appearance-design ability is adequate. And a luncheon meeting with someone from upper management, making sure the candidate knows the man's position, would allow the manager to *observe* the candidate's ability to deal with top-echelon people.

Managers frequently neglect this kind of informal evaluation, and yet it can be a most informative, persuasive source of information. It involves only a scrutiny of the specifications and some preplanning of things to ask a candidate to do that would display the ability or quality in question. In other words, don't just ask the candidate whether he can do something; place him in a situation in which he *shows* he can do it.

For other matters that do not readily yield to this kind of demonstration, a good standard interview of the employment type is needed. A number of very good books [3] are available that suggest patterns of questions for a manager to ask. Skill, of course, comes only with practice. But if a manager learns to ask broad enough questions that cannot easily be answered yes or no, and if he can see his role as one of a listener who merely

[3] See R. A. Fear, *The Evaluation Interview,* Second Edition, McGraw-Hill Book Company, New York, 1973; and Glenn A. Bassett, *Practical Interviewing,* AMACOM, New York, 1965.

keeps the candidate talking about accomplishments about which the manager wants elaboration, he will usually get the information he wants.

In any event, the personal interview will readily give the manager information about appearance, manner, and the kind of first impression the candidate makes. Since an interview, as normally set up, is a one-to-one situation, even this kind of information may be amplified by including, before the interview is over, other individuals—associates of the manager, prospective associates of the candidate—so as to get some understanding of how he handles himself in a group, assuming that meeting and working with groups is one of the job requirements.

If, at the end of the interview, the manager feels he has a qualified candidate and wants to do a little selling on the desirability of the organization, the work, and so on, he is then in a sound position to do so.

When the interview has been completed and the information and impressions have been digested along with other information gathered previously, the manager may need to go back to a former employer and review some of the points that now appear critical and about which information may be somewhat vague or contradictory.

Finally, on the basis of all the information obtained about all the candidates, the manager compares the apparent strength and deficiency of each candidate with each item of the specification (see Exhibit 8 for a useful format) and makes a judgmental decision that Candidate X appears best qualified and will be offered the position—provided, of course, he meets at least minimum standards. If not, the search starts over. Should X not accept the offer, Candidate Y will be offered the position next, and so on. This kind of systematic collection of information as a basis for appraising candidate qualifications against carefully detailed position and situational requirements substantially increases the manager's batting average in selecting excellent personnel.

A manager who has to fill an open position in his organization appraises first the knowledge, skill, and personal qualities required by the job. Second, he appraises the situational factors that make it easy or difficult to perform the work and translates these into additional required knowledge, skill, and personal qualities. He then investigates the extent to which candidates possess these abilities, using such sources as personnel records and résumés, evaluative judgments of former employers, formal and informal test data, and the impressions, interests, reported accomplishments, and personal qualities exhibited in a personal interview. Finally, he compares the relative strengths of candidates against the requirements and makes a judgmental decision as to who is best qualified and whether he meets at least minimum standards.

chapter 14

Making use of candidate appraisals

WHEN THE MANAGER HAS NOTIFIED A CANDIDATE THAT HE HAS "won the competition" for the open position and the candidate has accepted the offer, the manager often sighs with relief, gathers together his extensive notes on candidate qualifications, and sweeps them into his circular file. If he is an "enlightened" manager, he may give them to his secretary: "Here, Ann, put these somewhere. Bill reports next Monday, and I've got to get back to work." End of usefulness of these data and example of lost managerial opportunity.

For the company as a whole, the collected data represent needed information. Even for candidates from outside the company, the personnel department may be able to offer the accumulated data to other managers with open positions and save them considerable effort.

Certainly for a rejected candidate already employed in the company, the information represents a current snapshot of his strengths and deficiencies that should help his manager to set sound targets for coaching. In terms of career planning, it may be of invaluable help to both employee and manager in evolving developmental experiences.

For the rejected candidate himself, a few moments with his boss or, if he is willing, with the manager who did not accept him may be in order. The purpose is to review those deficiencies that the manager felt would have been detrimental and those areas where other candidates had more to offer. This will provide the person with information to update his self-appraisal of his performance and his career goals and will give him an opportunity to make or renew personal decisions.

Of primary importance to the manager, however, is that the data he has collected about the successful candidate afford him an opportunity to make an immediate, positive contribution to the productivity and effectiveness of the new incumbent. This careful, detailed appraisal of the man's abilities to do the work in the setting in which it needs to be done provides the basis for coaching and performance improvement that should begin the very day the man appears on the job.

There must have been certain assets that from the manager's viewpoint were the overriding reasons for choosing this person. Step 1 for the manager is to make sure that these are put to work immediately. Perhaps the easiest way is to select a few short-range goals that represent essential work of high priority, that especially involve use of the employee's talents, and that do not place too much demand on unknown or weaker abilities. For example, if an employee is hired as a field service engineer and the biggest plus in his background is an intimate knowledge of the product coupled with strong practical engineering know-how, early assignments might well be of the troubleshooting variety rather than a series of get-acquainted customer calls, especially if the ability to communicate with others is not one of the engineer's strong points.

Concurrently, the manager needs to identify knowledge gaps and have a very specifically detailed plan for filling in these gaps. Not to be overlooked is information about the firm and, if he is a newcomer, the organization in which the man will now be working; information about systems, processes, methods, paperwork, and the like; and business goals and strategy that might affect early actions and decisions. If the manager does not want to place himself in the position of supplying this information, he may help the person identify what he needs to know and where, in or out of the company, it is available so that the employee can dig it out for himself.

Finally, to deal with skill deficiencies and inexperience in the face of certain situational factors, the manager must make plans in advance that will help the employee strengthen such areas over a reasonable period of time. Ways of doing this are discussed in Chapter 5.

Doing these things—focusing the employee initially on parts of the job for which he is well qualified, working out ways he can acquire the information he needs, and evolving somewhat longer-range plans for performance improvement on the basis of preselection appraisal information—all contribute to more effective transition and more rapid productivity.

There is something in this for the manager personally, too. As a manager, one of the critical things he must do is to employ people who are able to carry out the work of the organization extremely well. Indeed, selecting qualified individuals is the most important way in which he can meet the expectations of his own manager. So it is important that this managerial skill be developed and improved over the years. The usual learning steps apply:

1. *Set a learning goal.* The manager consciously sets as his target the improvement of his ability to pick excellent employees to fill open positions.

2. *Provide the necessary information.* The manager gets

whatever help is available from the personnel department, reads books on the subject so that he is aware of the problems and the tools available to him, and so on.

3. *Afford an opportunity to apply the information.* The manager has this opportunity each time an open position occurs on his staff.

4. *Supply timely and useful feedback.* This is where the documented appraisal material collected prior to the employment of the new hire comes into use. The manager recorded his appraisal of the job requirements, the situational or environmental requirements, and his judgments about the employee's capability in each of these areas. As the employee takes over in the job and begins working toward needed goals, the manager can record what the work and situational requirements actually are and how the employee stacks up with respect to needed knowledge, skill, and personal qualities. Did the manager predict the employee's performance correctly? Was his estimate of the work, the situation, and the man's abilities correct? Where he was correct, on what information had he based his judgment and what was its source? What tools had he used to obtain it—personal interview, informal testing, or demonstration? Where he was wrong, on what information had he based his judgment, and what sources and tools had he used? Why the error? What should he do differently the next time? This kind of feedback is much needed if the manager is to improve his skill next time around.

It is important to note that sometimes the manager's estimate of the man's abilities is correct but the situation changes drastically subsequent to employment. Or the manager badly over- or underestimates the work requirements and the man cannot meet the more demanding levels. These are cases of managerial failure rather than employee failure to meet expectations. Unfortunately, failure on *either* side leads to inevitable distress for both parties when action is taken to correct the situation. For this reason the manager needs to be sensitive to changes on all three fronts—the work, the situation, and the employee's performance—and to factor foreseeable changes into his plans as quickly as possible.

Information from candidate appraisals serves a number of purposes. It helps the employment office identify other positions within the organization for which the candidate might be considered (or eliminates him from consideration if this appears to be more suitable). If the candidate is already an employee, information transmitted to him by his manager or by the manager who failed to hire him may permit more objective self-evaluation. Further, candidate appraisal offers the manager a basis for working out an initial performance improvement plan for the employee so that he is quickly effective in his new position. And finally, it provides meaningful feedback on the manager's skill in selection, thus permitting him to adapt and improve this critical capability.

chapter 15

Organizing the appraisal system

TODAY'S MODERN MANAGER IS FACED WITH THE NEED TO MAKE a variety of appraisals: to help an employee improve his performance, to recommend appropriate salary action, to estimate an individual's potential, to select a qualified candidate to fill an opening. Each of these important appraisal situations is by itself complex and time consuming. How can a manager remember to consider all the "right" factors? How can he be sure he has laid reasonable groundwork for an activity that could otherwise be disturbing to employees? Most important, how can he be sure to collect information over an extended period of time so that when he is called upon for a judgment based on a study of representative information he will have the facts at hand and not need to start from scratch?

In today's dynamic business atmosphere, a manager needs to be prepared to make judgments and decisions with very little advance notification. This is not a signal for snap decisions. Decisions and recommendations are lived with for a long time and should be rooted in factual data, realistically considered. So the time that the decision is needed is seldom the time to *begin* collecting information on which to base it. At most, there is opportunity to update and review data; reflect upon, analyze, and weigh information; and come to a conclusion.

It is especially important that respect for human values be a major factor in arriving at the decision. Mistakes involving people are not easily corrected, and ethical principles demand constant awareness of and sympathy for the other person's welfare, both immediate and long-term.

What follows, therefore, is a system of practices and records that will help assure managerial readiness for decisions and recommendations that affect employees. Two forms (Exhibits 1 and 2) are fundamental to all the appraisal instruments shown. They document what the employee commits himself to accomplish and what he in fact accomplishes. To this basic information, then, the managers add whatever other information or estimate they need in order to serve specific purposes such as coaching, salary recommendations, evaluations of potential, and so on. What is recommended is not the only system, of course, and infinite variations adapted to the style of the manager are possible. The suggested forms are quite secondary in importance and are only a starting point, a way to begin documenting information so that it is readily accessible when it is needed. As managers gain experience in collecting, recording, and using such data, they will want to alter the formats to suit their own purposes.

RECORDING EMPLOYEE APPRAISALS

Candidate accepts offer of position. The manager starts a personnel file for the employee if he does not already have one from a previous job. Into it go a brief description of the position or a list of major assigned responsibilities and an organization chart showing the way this position fits with others in the department. Into it also go the specifications against which the employee was selected together with the summary of his qualifications and deficiencies for the position and the manager's action plan for eliminating some of these deficiencies. (See Chapter 14 and Exhibit 8.)

Employee comes on the job. The responsibilities of the position, the way the work fits in the department, and the initial assignments need thorough review and discussion with the employee not once but several times during the first three to six months. Obviously the amount of discussion will depend on the experience and maturity of the employee and whether he is new to the firm, to the department, to the manager, or only to the position he now fills. Chapters 5 and 14 cover the highlights of managerial action required here.

During this period the manager will want to be sure the employee understands the minimum and maximum salary for his work, the ground rules for salary increases, and any standard personnel practices that might affect him. He should also make clear his personal philosophy of managing and his personal expectations with respect to working with the employee. This is a period in which the two people are getting to know each other, and it is critical to developing a sound working relationship.

If the manager errs in his communication during this period, it is well to err on the side of providing more information than the employee needs, being more explicit than necessary in giving assignments and more definite in describing how he expects things to be handled. Most managers underestimate what the employee needs, and most new employees fail to ask all the things they should—lest they display their ignorance.

Into the manager's personnel file should go each of the major assignments given during this orientation period together with his notes on how well the employee performs, whether or not he displays the qualities that were anticipated when he was being considered for the position, and any new information that comes to light about his capabilities. See Exhibit 1 and 3.

Steady-state condition. Once the manager feels he has an awareness of the employee's capabilities and ways of accomplishing results and the employee is able to get around in the organization on his own, the two settle down to a normal give-and-take kind of daily working relationship. (See Chapter 4 on feedback.) Use of the work planning and progress review method of delegation is recommended. (See Chapter 6.) Employee and manager agree on goals and plans for accomplishing them, and these are put in writing and placed in the employee's folder, as shown in Exhibit 1. As progress is or is not made, the employee briefs the manager, who makes notes of key changes in work plans. Together they look at problems and obstacles and ways of getting work back on schedule. Into the personnel file go notes on their action plan, its implementation, and the degree of success in accomplishing what they set out to do.

At the end of the work-planning period, the employee's accomplishments are summarized together with a description of any conditions that made the accomplishments noteworthy. (See Exhibit 2.) For inexperienced employees, this summary might be made every six months. For mature, seasoned professionals, once a year or at the conclusion of a major project is probably a more suitable time.

Whenever the manager feels it appropriate or the employee requests it (but certainly at the time the accomplishment summary is made), the manager makes a coaching appraisal. (See Exhibit 3.) As a result, he selects one or more coaching methods (see Chapter 5) tailored to the situation faced. These decisions and resulting actions become part of the record, too.

Salary appraisal and action. Periodically, depending on the philosophy and practices of the firm, the manager needs to consider the employee's salary and make a recommendation with respect to it. He might use a form like Exhibit 4 to record information collected for the appraisal and note any unusual reaction when the employee is notified. His notes also go into the employee's file.

Recapitulation. The manager now has at hand a statement of the employee's total work responsibility, his assets and deficiencies for the work as evaluated prior to his appointment, and a detailed record of the results he has been asked to accomplish and the extent to which he has been able to do so, factoring in the general situation or environment in which he has been working. In addition, the manager has notes of developmental actions he has initiated and the way in which the employee has responded. With this information he is in a very favorable position to consider, after an appropriate interval, the employee's possible advancement if this seems warranted, his termination if it appears he cannot perform the work within a reasonable time, or powerful performance improvement activities if they are needed in certain work areas.

Employee potential and career. Chapters 11 and 12 describe managerial activity in these areas. All notes of appraisal, points for discussion, and action plans go into the employee's personnel file. See Exhibits 5, 6, and 7.

Employee termination. Chapter 10 covers this circumstance, and Exhibits 1 and 3 provide a format for recording information for the record.

Performance improvement. See Chapters 4 through 7. Exhibits 1, 2, and 3 provide a way of continuing to record this information.

Employee promotion. If, finally, a better opening occurs for which the employee may be considered qualified, the manager has at hand a wealth of information that can be made available for consideration against the specifications of the position to be filled. (See Chapter 13.) If the employee is accepted for the new position, the manager begins again with the new employee who comes to take his place. If he is not accepted, the manager seizes the opportunity to review with the employee the reasons why he was not accepted so that they may either incorporate these into the employee's developmental action plans or change his career goals appropriately.

SUMMARY

Throughout his working relationship with the employee, then, the manager is subjecting himself to the discipline of recording the major facts he learns about the employee's abilities and his response to new challenges. This need not be an elaborate system of record keeping but should be a running record, quite likely handwritten, of factual information about specific achievements against assigned goals together with enough information about the situation to indicate whether accomplishment was easy or hard. It contains notes about actions the manager takes in his effort to contribute to the employee's development, how the employee responds, and what he feels are his long-term career interests. It also contains information on the extent to which the manager was able to reward both accomplishment and development in monetary and other ways. The intent of the record is not to hang the employee but rather to insure that the manager makes the soundest, fairest decisions possible on the basis of sufficient representative, relevant information.

How long should such a record be retained, and should it follow the employee if he moves on to another manager? Factual information is always up to date; it is the judgments, guesses, estimates that become obsolete. So send along the facts—the employee's education, his assignments, his accomplishments, changes in accomplishment both good and bad, salary data, and similar items—but omit the guesses, the judgmental comments, the estimate of potential. Let the new manager make his own estimate from the documented facts. He may, after all, have different standards or values. He will undoubtedly weight various performance factors quite differently; indeed, the new job may *require* a different weighting of these factors.

Occasionally employees feel the differences in managers are somehow unfair or unjust. Actually these differences in ways of getting results often represent developmental opportunities for employees and stimulate whole new patterns of performance. And it should be remembered that the methods described here for working with an employee and for documenting managerial action and employee response do not constitute a *rigid* system of appraisal. Instead the manager should think about it in the light of his own personality and should view the methods, the processes, the forms as aids to his understanding, examples of *how* to make an appraisal, and then take action. In each area he should keep in mind the fundamental principles, focus on what he is trying to do, and then ask himself: ''Is this way the best one for me and for this employee—or is there another way that would accomplish the same result and be better for me at this time and under these conditions?''

On the other hand, a new way sometimes seems harder than an old one because of its unfamiliarity. So a manager who is trying to improve his own skills should be willing to experiment a little, to try a different approach long enough to get over the hurdle of newness and evaluate its possible contribution to his own ability to get results.

The fundamental questions in employee appraisal are:
☐ Why do I need this appraisal—what is its purpose?
☐ What factors are fundamentally related to this purpose?
☐ What information do I have on these factors?
☐ Is the available information sufficient, relevant, and representative so that I can make a sound judgmental decision?
☐ What is the most helpful and effective action I can take as a result of my appraisal?

Recognition of these fundamental questions will prohibit use of an all-purpose employee appraisal system for the same reason that a ruler in a workman's kit is not used to measure everything from board width to fine wire size. Managers will instead begin to select with sensitivity the particular appraisal tool they need to make the particular appraisal that is called for. They will, with practice, increase the skill with which they apply the appropriate instrument and the innovation with which they plan their subsequent action.

chapter 16

Questions frequently asked about appraisal

QUESTION: PERSONALITY IS OFTEN A MAJOR FACTOR IN AN employee's failure to do his job, so why shouldn't a manager or supervisor talk to him about it?

Answer: It is true that personality affects performance both favorably and unfavorably. The point is, however, that the employee is not usually able to change his basic personality very much, nor is a manager often competent to help him do it. If together they can pinpoint specific behavior that is creating problems on the job, they can talk about these, attempt to work out more acceptable ways of behaving, try them out to see if they help, and modify them as needed.

So don't ignore personality; instead, focus attention

where there's likely to be payoff—specific performance activity; specific work results; specific work habits, specific work methods; specific employee ways of behaving, speaking, gesticulating. These can usually be narrowed down sufficiently to reach understanding with an employee and, with a little discipline and effort from both manager and employee, acceptable substitutes can be developed and put into practice that will have a favorable impact on the employee's work.

Question: It has been our practice to discuss improvements in performance and the employee's development plans at the same time we tell him whether or not he has earned a salary increase. Is this wrong?

Answer: It isn't a question of right or wrong. The question is: Is this the most effective way for a manager to motivate an employee to improve his performance and stimulate him to take action for his personal growth?

If the discussion precedes the salary notification so that the employee feels his salary may be at stake, he will often try to explain why he did not do all the things expected of him. He will be on the defensive, so to speak, and it will be more than usually difficult to help him think constructively about his future work and career.

On the other hand, if the discussion follows the salary notification, the employee often becomes absorbed in thinking about the increase—what he will do with it, whether it is more or less than he expected—and it is frankly difficult to capture his full attention and focus it on future work.

If the discussion follows notification that there will be no increase for the time being, the emotions of the employee —whether anger, resentment, regret, or resignation—are usually not a good basis for immediate discussion of corrective actions.

So the prudent manager, having notified the employee of his salary decision with a brief explanation of his reasons, postpones for at least a short time the "What will we do about it?'' discussion, thus giving the employee a brief adjustment period.

Employee reaction is an individual matter, of course, so practices should be adjusted to what is known about the employee. In general, however, the chances of getting constructive thinking are increased if an adjustment period intervenes before this critical discussion is tackled—if, indeed, it is decided that this is the best way to effect improvement. See Chapter 5 for other ways.

Question: In an earlier chapter you describe ''Work Planning and Review.'' How does this differ from ''Management by Objectives''?

Answer: It is quite similar in philosophy but places more emphasis on frequent review of short-term results and re-examination of forward plans. It also stresses enrichment of innovative or improvement objectives by describing the main elements of action plans designed to achieve them. Thus it provides the manager with clear coaching opportunities and an early warning system for his decision making. A negotiated psychological contract between an employee and manager is recommended in ''Work Planning and Review.'' It is not necessarily a part of ''Management by Objectives.''

Question: If a manager sets goals with an employee at the beginning of the year, does his day-to-day coaching faithfully, and has several reviews with the employee either individually or in a group to see how the work is progressing, does he need to hold a formal once-a-year appraisal discussion in addition?

Answer: Never hold a discussion *just* to have held it. First decide what is to be accomplished. If it is performance improvement, there are probably better ways of doing this, as detailed in Chapter 5. If it is to summarize evidence of performance failure and notify the employee he must improve or be fired, it had better be held. If the intent is to summarize where work stands as a basis for making next year's work plans and budgets, it should be held and will probably get better results if much of the discussion is employee-generated. If it is to tell an employee why a certain salary decision was made, it should be held, but it should be kept brief.

The important thing is to decide what is to be accomplished with the employee and then choose the most effective means for doing it.

Question: Most behavioral scientists agree that development occurs on the job as a result of the ongoing relationship between employee and manager. Why, then, do you stress a periodic coaching appraisal for this purpose?

Answer: Ideally managers should be able to establish the kind of climate or environment for employees that helps them want to grow. But we must recognize that some are far better at doing this than others. And some *think* they are better than they really are. In addition, interest in self-development may be necessary but it may not be enough for growth, especially accelerated growth. There are times when it is vital for an employee to see what to grow toward; that is, what directions for growth are most needed by the organization. There are also times when a manager needs to think through ways of restructuring the environment in tangible ways (through organization change, addition of resources, improvement of procedures and work systems) in order to help the employee achieve greater growth. I am not underestimating the importance of relationship and climate. I commend them and more, too. A thoughtful coaching appraisal can help a manager arrive at priorities: Is it primarily the environment that needs upgrading? Or are there some positive actions he should take as well to clarify direction and facilitate accomplishment? And which comes first?

Question: To what extent should the appraisal for salary determination also consider the employee's probable potential?

Answer: Companies have different philosophies on this point, but regardless of philosophy, potential is actually considered indirectly in a number of ways.

First of all, the employee who has high potential is probably advancing more rapidly than others, so he is often already in a position that permits a higher maximum for him than for some of his associates. Second, his high potential is usually recognized *because* he is doing an outstanding job on his present assignment. Consideration for increase is therefore more likely. Third, his market value outside the company is probably higher than that of others with less future. Fourth, his individual situation is probably such that he is considered more favorably because of the desire to retain his competence in the organization. So in at least these four ways potential is considered and has a favorable impact on salary considerations.

One problem arises if the employee is moved laterally in the organization to give him broad experience in several important kinds of work. He may already be paid more than the going rate for a job he should learn to do. For example, he may be paid more than the maximum for a foreman, and yet this is experience he needs for later advancement. An enlightened manager or development program administrator will, in selected cases, ignore the established salary range and adjust the pay situation to the individual case, considering any temporary overpayment to be an investment that the employee's excellent performance and later contribution will justify. When this is not possible to do within the framework of salary policies, frank discussion with the employee may help him see a temporary cut in pay as an investment in his future.

Question: Should appraisal and salary be discussed together?

Answer: Yes. The manager needs to tell the employee in a general way, and briefly, why he did or did not recommend a salary increase. (See Chapter 9.)

If, however, the question is whether the manager should

discuss how the employee can improve his performance at the same time he discusses salary with him, the answer, generally speaking, is no. It is better to reserve this discussion for another time, one more conducive to constructive thinking.

Question: Should management consultants evaluate or appraise executives for top-echelon positions?

Answer: There is a distinction between taking action based on a decision and collecting the information used for the decision. A manager with an opening should take personal responsibility for deciding who will fill it. Only in this way can he be held responsible for the performance of the organization he manages.

If he recognizes in himself certain blind spots or a lack of skill in determining candidate qualifications or position requirements, there is no reason why he should not employ specialists to help him develop these data. Probably he often asks an accountant to help compile cost figures for his scrutiny or market research specialists to prepare consumer survey data. In much the same fashion he might ask an employment specialist, a psychologist, or a management consultant to provide candidates, compile data about their qualifications, or analyze the demands of the open position.

True, because he is dealing with a human being he needs to exercise special care in the safeguarding of such information, the use he makes of it, and the thoughtfulness with which he considers it. He will also want to assure himself of the competence and accuracy of the person who supplies the data and, as with other kinds of analyses, to double-check critical points himself. Beyond this, however, the specialized help such individuals are able to give is frequently invaluable, particularly if the manager cannot be truly objective, perhaps because he is personally involved in some way.

The basic points to keep in mind are that the manager carry the responsibility for being sure that he has sufficient accurate, representative, and relevant information (regardless of its source), that he weigh it with care, and that he make the best judgmental decision within his power to make.

Question: When should a manager deliberately seek the help of others in making employee appraisals?

Answer: He should do this whenever he does not have enough accurate, representative, relevant information at hand and needs the input of one or more others. For example, for a new employee he undoubtedly needs input from former managers. He should also do this whenever he suspects he has some personal bias or prejudice that will not permit him to weigh information with reasonable objectivity.

He should always do it when he is so involved in a situation that he is himself a major factor to be considered. For example, in estimating environmental conditions in which one of his employees works, he probably cannot be fully objective about the effect of his own managing style on those who report to him. And he probably needs help from a third party if he believes his relationships with employees are deteriorating.

It is reasonably certain that one appraisal area in which a manager needs the contribution of others is in estimating an employee's potential. The consensus of several persons who know the employee and have seen him in a variety of situations adds to the validity of the conclusions.

A second specific evaluation usually requires the input of others. This is in the relationships area. A manager probably sees first hand only the handling of the upward relationship. For data on dealings with associates, customers, and those supervised, he had better collect first-hand information from others.

Question: We have been told that our appraisal discussions with employees should be completely frank. Do you agree with this?

Answer: Yes and no. Yes, in the sense that what is discussed with an employee should be a true expression of the manager's opinion. No, in the sense that a manager probably should not discuss *all* his opinions with the employee. Appreciation of human values and insight into one's personal limitations should limit discussion to those shortcomings of real importance to the employee's current job or opportunity for advancement. And if a manager expects the employee to change in some way, he is wise to limit discussion and attention to only one or two items that are within the employee's ability to control.

Question: Should we be softer in appraising performance and potential of minority employees and women so that they get a better break in salary and promotion recommendations?

Answer: This is a pretty unrealistic approach. We should, in fact, be tougher on ourselves in analyzing incisively what they do well and badly. We should accelerate their capabilities to do current jobs well and to accept greater responsibility at appropriate times. We do no one a favor if we mislead her or him by soft feedback. On the other hand, this does not mean we should overwhelm someone with criticism or discuss needed change with brutality. A supportive, helpful attitude combined with high expectations and clear, explicit feedback on high-priority issues is the most promising approach.

Question: Should a manager be willing to change his appraisal as a result of an employee's reaction during discussion?

Answer: If a manager chooses to discuss his appraisal of some aspect of an employee's work and future, he should expect some sort of response. If this response brings information into the picture that is relevant to the appraisal purpose and that the manager has *not* considered previously or given proper weight, he should be willing to factor it into his judgment. And if it affects his judgment one way or the other, he should be willing to change his overall appraisal decision.

Unless the manager did a careless job in assembling

information earlier, this situation does not reflect discredit on him. In fact, his willingness to consider all pertinent information and react appropriately is much to his credit.

A problem presumably occurs if the change in the manager's overall judgment requires notification of his own boss. If no procedure is available for doing this, one good way of handling it is to staple to the original appraisal form a memo containing the new information and the change it makes in the summary judgment, then red-pencil the change onto the original appraisal.

Question: Should an employee be asked to do an independent appraisal of his work performance?

Answer: Yes, frequently. However, whether he should be asked to discuss it with his manager depends on—

□ Clear agreement between them on the work factors to be appraised.

□ Employee understanding of the manager's standards; that is, what are considered to be the criteria or ground rules for successful accomplishment of the work he is expected to perform.

□ Good communication between them on how these factors are to be measured.

□ What the manager hopes to accomplish.

If the intent is to see how much insight the employee has into his performance assets and liabilities, it is a good system. If it is to give him a feeling of self-responsibility for his work, it is a good system. But if the manager is going to fire the employee for nonperformance, it is not such a good idea. (See Chapter 10.)

Question: If you were to give a single suggestion to help minority employees and women advance themselves, what would it be?

Answer: Choose jobs that are well defined and highly measurable so that you and your boss are constantly in a position to know how well you are doing and difference of opinion is unlikely.

Question: How does a manager appraise the performance of a specialist who knows more about his field than the manager does?

Answer: This is a case in which the use of a third person may be very desirable. If there is available within the firm someone of stature in the employee's field of specialization, perhaps he can be called upon to review the employee's work and give his opinions to the manager. If there is no one within the company, perhaps occasionally a reputable expert from a university or consulting firm can play the same role. In the latter case the manager needs to be careful to add his own judgment about the employee's contribution to the business or to the organization, since someone on the outside probably does not have this perspective. In this case, too, setting clear, specific, measurable results for the employee to obtain will help both the manager and the employee to know whether they have been achieved. Self-appraisal on the part of the employee would also be useful in this instance.

Question: Should an employee have a copy of his current performance appraisal for his later reference?

Answer: There are both advantages and disadvantages to this. The question implies, however, that discussion of appraisal will always occur, and this is not necessarily the case. (See Chapter 5.) If the appraisal is discussed, some of the *advantages* of letting the employee have a copy are these:

    ☐ It lets him review the content privately, without stress, and reflect on it by himself.

    ☐ Seeing the appraisal sheet itself takes some of the mystery out of the situation.

    ☐ It eliminates some ethical problems. It is less likely

that there will be written material in the record that the employee knows nothing about.

Some of the *disadvantages,* on the other hand, are these:

☐ In reviewing the sheet by himself, without the manager's accompanying oral explanation, there is danger of unfavorable employee reaction because of misinterpretation.

☐ The employee may put too much effort on correcting the negative points at the expense of other more favorable points it would be desirable to develop.

☐ As time goes by, the information, wording, and the like grow stale and the remarks are reinterpreted in ways the manager never intended.

Some managers suggest that the employee make notes during the discussion of any points to be remembered or acted upon. Then at least the words are his, and they may carry less import later and are less likely to be misinterpreted.

In today's open society, however, if the appraisal document is going into the employee's record, it is almost unthinkable that the employee should not be given a copy or at least offered one if he chooses to take it. So rapidly is this trend growing in North America today that in spite of the disadvantages noted above, we must answer yes.

Question: How far ahead do you believe it is wise for an employee to set career goals?

Answer: Set career goals for any period of time—but keep flexibility so that as new opportunities appear attractive, an individual does not find himself locked into a future he no longer wants or considers relatively less desirable. To foster a good balance between having a direction for one's life and staying open to alternatives, do more than just set ultimate goals. In addition, determine a reasonable next step and approximately when it should be taken. This shorter-term focus should then trigger a review of ultimate goals at the time the next step is to be taken and adjustments made in the light of the total situation at that time.

Question: If a manager honestly does not feel able to help an employee make sound decisions about his career, but the employee asks him for help, what should he do?

Answer: First he should see and talk to the employee informally to find out what he has in mind. Maybe he has just had another job offer and wants to tell the manager about it. Maybe he feels discouraged about his work and wants to get his feelings off his chest. Maybe he is particularly upset or disturbed by some recent occurrence and needs to let off steam. Just by being a good listener the manager may provide a needed outlet.

If the employee does want help or advice with his career planning, the manager should tell him quite simply that he does not feel able to help on this and fears any comments or advice he could offer would be valueless. He should then refer the man to his own boss (if this has been arranged previously) or to a qualified member of the personnel department or an outside vocational counselor. With the employee's consent he can display his support and positive interest by calling the person to whom he refers the employee *in the employee's presence*, explaining the situation as best he can and telling him that the employee will call to arrange a mutually convenient time.

Question: While few managers will admit to doing this, if an employee who is not particularly strong is being considered for another position, they do the best they can to sell the man to the new manager. This is so unfair! What can be done about it?

Answer: Yes, it is unfair—unfair to the employee who goes into another position for which he is doubtfully qualified; unfair to the manager who trusts the former manager's word and now gets poorer-than-expected performance; unfair to the firm that now must live with unsatisfactory performance for another indefinite period.

The probability that this will occur is diminished if the hiring manager follows the procedure outlined in Chapter 13 and focuses on exactly what the employee has been assigned to do and what result he has achieved in doing it, rather than asking the manager if the employee can do the open job.

The problem is a little bigger than this, however. Some managers really do not want to be unfair or to hurt anyone. It simply seems to them that a new job will change everything for the employee. And every once in a while things work out just this way. Given a new manager, new work, and a whole new situation, the previously failing employee improves dramatically. Perhaps one day the social scientists will help us understand why this happens and, more importantly, how we can help it happen.

exhibits

IT HAS BEEN SUGGESTED THROUGHOUT THESE PAGES THAT managers keep records as one part of the appraisal process. The exhibits that follow will serve as guides for the gathering, ordering, and storing of the data managers need to help them appraise effectively. It should be remembered, however, that these are not fixed and rigid formats. They should be adapted to suit individual needs and set up in such a way that there will be plenty of space for recording all the necessary information. Don't try to crowd your notes in too small a space lest you omit points that may later prove to be critical to your decision.

It should also be remembered that quality appraisals and implementation are the objectives—not the completion of forms, which merely remind managers of decisions made and yet to be made and encourage them to take appropriate action.

EXHIBIT 1
BASIC RECORD OF PERFORMANCE

Employee: _____ Period of work: _____ to _____

Employee's position: _____ Manager: _____

PART A: CONTINUING RESPONSIBILITIES

| | Budgets and Standards | *Actual Performance* | | | |
		1st Qtr.	2nd Qtr.	3rd Qtr.	4th Qtr.
1.					
2.					
3.					
(etc.)					

PART B: MAJOR GOALS, INVOLVING PROGRAMS AND PROJECTS

	Man-hours		Person Respon- sible	Begin Date		End Date		Notes and Comments (Performance Ground Rules, Anticipated Obstacles, Resources Allowed, Progress Review Dates)
	Est.	Act.		Est.	Act.	Est.	Act.	

Goal 1:
   Task (a)
   Task (b)
   Task (c)
   (etc.)

Goal 2:
   Task (a)
   Task (b)
   Task (c)
   (etc.)

When progress is reviewed, preferably indicate planned revisions on the original, using colored pencil to highlight.

EXHIBIT 2
Employee Accomplishment Summary

Employee: _____   Period of work: ___ to _____

Position: _____   Date of summary: _____

Manager: _____

(This may be completed by either the employee or the manager as long as both agree it fairly reflects the employee's accomplishments during the stated period.)

Accomplishment versus Agreed-on Results	*Factors Contributing to Ease or Difficulty of Accomplishment*
1.	
2.	
3.	
4.	
5.	

EXHIBIT 3
Coaching Appraisal Summary

Employee: _____ Future period
of work: _____ to _____

Position: _____ Date of coaching

Manager: _____ appraisal: _____

Manager refers to Exhibit 1 (and to Exhibit 2, if available) for this employee and considers the following items:

1. What areas of employee's work are going well?

2. What areas of employee's work need strengthening during the next six to twelve months?

3. What future events outside the employee's control may affect, positively or negatively, the employee's ability to accomplish planned results during the next six to twelve months?

4. What significant strengths has employee demonstrated on this or previous jobs which should be fully used during the next six to twelve months?

5. What significant gaps in knowledge or experience, what skill development needs or behavior modifications appear desirable for the employee to improve his work during the next six to twelve months? (Limit to a very few high-priority items, not more than 2 or 3.)

(*Exhibit 3 continued*)

Based on consideration of the above items, summarize coaching decisions:

   A. Manager will do the following (indicate timing):

   B. Manager will recommend that the employee take the following actions (indicate timing):

   C. Date for manager to check progress or reevaluate coaching needs:

EXHIBIT 4
SALARY APPRAISAL SUMMARY

Employee: _____

Position: _____   Current salary: _____

Length of
time in position: _____   Current min. and
                                       max. for position: _____

1. Major employee performance contributions (consult Exhibits 1 and 2):

2. Paid salaries of firm's comparable employees (consult salary administrator):

3. Market value of employee's work (consult salary administrator):

4. Individual's past and current salary treatment (consult individual's salary history):

5. Administrative, legal, and business considerations:

Salary decision: _____per ____beginning _____
                                                        Date

or

No increase now. Review again: _____
                                          Date

Summary of reasons for decision:

Signed _____

Date of salary appraisal _____

Employee notified: _____
                                     Date

203

EXHIBIT 5
ESTIMATE OF EMPLOYEE POTENTIAL

Employee: _____   Length of time

Position: _____   employee has reported

to manager: _____

Manager: _____   Date of appraisal: _____

(Since one person's judgment in estimating another's potential is often inaccu-
rate, managers are urged to seek opinions of others who know the person's work
and through discussion try to reach a consensus. Managers are also urged to
consider potential in the light of the employee's desires for himself. Certainly
action taken as a result of such an appraisal should be in consonance with the
employee's wishes and with his expressed consent. Consult Exhibit 7 if available.)

Summary of major demonstrated performance strengths:

Summary of major demonstrated performance deficiencies (indicate whether
probably improvable with reasonable effort):

Major trends in performance noted during past two or three years:

Estimated potential abilities not yet demonstrated at work (indicate basis for
estimate):

Probable growth as a manager (indicate basis for estimate):

Probable growth as an individual worker (indicate basis for estimate):

Career recommendations of former managers, professional vocational counselor, personnel development specialist, or others:

Employee's stated career interests:

Manager's estimate of probable top positions employee may achieve in company:

Joint manager–employee recommendation of desirable next positions for employee:

Joint manager–employee list of employee's three most needed skills, performance improvements, or developmental experiences to achieve next positions:

Note: Be specific. Avoid generalities and broad adjectives. Review at least annually.

EXHIBIT 6
Runner-up Chart

Manager—ABC Department Present Incumbent (Age)		
Candidate 1	Age	Color Code
Candidate 2	Age	Color Code
Candidate 3	Age	Color Code

Position A Present Incumbent (Age)		
Candidate 1	Age	Color Code
Candidate 2	Age	Color Code
Candidate 3	Age	Color Code

Position C Present Incumbent (Age)		
Candidate 1	Age	Color Code
Candidate 2	Age	Color Code
Candidate 3	Age	Color Code

Position B Present Incumbent (Age)		
Candidate 1	Age	Color Code
Candidate 2	Age	Color Code
Candidate 3	Age	Color Code

Submitted by _____

Date _____

Color Code:
Green—ready now.
Blue—ready in 1 to 2 years.
Red—ready in 3 to 5 years.
White—not likely to be qualified, but best available.

Note: Should be supplemented by recommendations of experience, training, etc., needed for readiness at stated time. Should represent a consensus of the views of several persons who know the persons named.

EXHIBIT 7
Guide for Manager and Employee in Preparation
For Career-Counseling Session

Employee _____

Manager _____

Date prepared _____

1. *Performance talents on which to build.* Consider work performed well, assignments most enjoyed, ways of getting results which represent strengths, favorable trends in performance, special fields of knowledge, demonstrated skills, functional strengths, off-the-job activities which indicate interests and potential abilities not yet shown at work, assets for managerial work, assets as an individual worker, etc. Consider also conditions under which these talents are usually demonstrated: pressure, amount and kind of supervision, freedom, etc.

2. *Performance deficiencies.* Consider failures in performance, assignments least enjoyed, ways of getting results which have unfavorable effects, unfavorable trends in performance, major knowledge and skill deficiencies, major functional experience deficiencies, deficiencies for managerial work, deficiencies for individual work, etc. Consider also conditions under which these deficiencies have been apparent: pressure, amount and kind of supervision, freedom, etc. (Circle items which could probably be improved readily.)

3. *Inputs from other managers, personnel specialists, vocational counselors, etc., about talents on which to build career.*

207

(Exhibit 7 continued)

4. *Future needs of company and important changes outside company that might affect career choice.* Consider: changes in economy, new industry, effects of automation, effects of internationalization, company's business plans and timing, need for new technologies, need for new managers and new ways of managing.

5. *Possible career directions.* Consider all fields: retail, industrial, government, social service, educational, publishing, etc.

Possible Future Positions	Required Additional Knowledge, Skill, Experience, Behavior Change

6. *List any questions to be discussed during the career-counseling session.*

EXHIBIT 8
APPRAISAL OF CANDIDATE QUALIFICATIONS

Principal Position Requirements	Information About Candidate 1		Information About Candidate 2		Information About Candidate 3	
	Item	Source	Item	Source	Item	Source
1.						
2.						
3.						
4.						

Decision:

Candidate brings these qualifications to the position:

Candidate will need help in these areas:

DATE DUE